BEGIN AGAIN

Discovering the New You after a Life-Changing Event

Pamala Bryant

For those struggling with self-love. There is still hope. You are not alone.

CONTENTS

Author's Note

This is the story of how I came to be diagnosed with lupus and how I chose to live life after my diagnosis. Having a non-curable illness doesn't have to be the end of your hopes and dreams. As I found out, it can be the beginning. I hope that the telling of my story will encourage and help others in their battles with disease and illness. No matter what life throws your way, you have the choice to wallow in self-pity or make things the best they can be. It's all about your mindset. If you choose to focus on the positive, no matter what else is happening, you will have a reason to smile. I know this is easier said than done, but as you'll discover in reading my book, it is something I've had to learn myself. So smile. Focus on the positive. Create new dreams for yourself. The best is yet to come!

PART I
BEING DIAGNOSED WITH LUPUS

Lupus—a chronic inflammatory condition caused by an autoimmune disease; it may cause depression, fatigue, hair loss, sensitivity to sunlight, and weight changes. LFA

Chapter 1:
The Nose Knows

"You have lupus."

Those are the three words I heard while walking from my doctor's office one afternoon in March 2007. After hearing the news, I smiled. I smiled because I finally knew what was wrong and how to make it better. I smiled because I no longer needed to be afraid of what my body was doing. I smiled because I felt like the worst of things was over.

Now I understand hearing you have a non-curable illness doesn't make most people happy. But to understand this happiness, you have to pause the imaginary tape player of my life and press rewind until you reach the summer of 2006. It was an exciting time in my life. I had just graduated from the University of Louisville with a Bachelor of Arts in English and was looking for a graduate program to transition into.

Getting degrees for my passions was something I decided was the best choice for me. I have always loved working with children and writing. Growing up, my sisters and I would babysit the kids in our neighborhood and during high school, we coached softball and tutored kids in an after-school program. We all have a love for guiding and nurturing children. My other passion is writing, which began in the fourth grade when I wrote my first paper entitled "Purple Skittles." I wrote about my fourth-grade teacher, Mrs. Lagerquest, who had left during the middle of the school year because of a brain aneurysm. I wrote about how, during recess, she would always have a bag of Skittles, and as some of my classmates and I walked with her, she would share her Skittles with us and save the purple ones for last. I knew then that I had a gift for writing, and I've been writing ever since! Therefore, I decided to complete my Master of Arts focusing on children. This way, I would have degrees for both of my passions, which meant I could find a job I loved after graduating.

So I knew I was going to graduate school, I knew what I'd study, and I knew I wasn't staying in Louisville. Growing up, I traveled every two to three years because my mom was in the Air Force, so I was used to moving and felt like I had stayed in Louisville long enough. Besides that, both my sisters and my mom had already moved away, so I had no real reason to stay. In addition to finding a school outside of the state, I also looked for a school that didn't require the GRE (I don't do well on standardized tests) and one that was very diverse.

I wanted a diverse school because in Louisville, you either hung out with whites or blacks. I didn't like it. Before moving to Louisville, I lived on military bases and had many friends of all nationalities. My sisters and I made friends quickly because we knew we only had a few years with them before we would have to move again. And when we picked our friends, we picked kids we thought were nice. It was never based on skin color.

However, when I moved to Louisville in eighth grade, all of that changed. I was now surrounded by mostly white and black students at school, and I lived in a black neighborhood. Gone were the days when I lived on base in a safe neighborhood where everyone knew each other, and I was allowed to play outside until it was dark. Now, I wasn't really allowed to hang out at my friends' houses or stay out until dark. I was even forbidden to go to some parts of the neighborhood. Still, it wasn't just my new surroundings. I was having a hard time fitting in.

Most of the students had lived in Louisville their whole lives and had made friends back in elementary school, so it was tough finding a group that would let me join them. The white students didn't want to hang out with me because I was black, and the black students didn't consider me fully black because of my light skin, long hair, and because I "talked like a white person." High school was a little better for me because I ran track and excelled in band, so I made friends that had the same interests as me.

I remember being so excited about undergrad. I wanted to have diverse friends again and have new experiences. I was confident that would happen in college. I completed mission work in St. Louis. I sang as a first soprano in the Black Diamond Gospel Choir and was a leader in one of the Christian organizations on campus. I even tried out for the rowing team! However, the same barrier regarding my race was present at the University of Louisville. So I just knew I had to get out of the South for grad school to have some hope of bringing diversity back into my life.

In my college search, I did notice some HBCUs, Historically Black Colleges and Universities that looked interesting. I liked some aspects of Fisk University in Tennessee, Clark Atlanta University in Georgia, and Grambling State University in Louisiana. Ultimately, though, I decided against an HBCU. I visited my sister on Howard University's campus for the past two years during homecoming. Even though I loved the soul food, I wasn't fond of attending a school where the females dressed up in makeup and heels for 8 am classes. That was too much pressure for me! I continued researching colleges to find my best fit, and that was when I came across New York University, NYU.

I have to admit it was love at first sight. I loved where the campus was located in Manhattan, the small classroom sizes, and the School Counseling program. I also loved the idea of living in New York, going to plays on Broadway and finding fabulous shopping deals. Checking what was required to apply, I realized that besides filling out forms and sending my grades, all I had to do was submit an essay as to why I wanted to go to NYU! I thought to myself, "Piece of cake!" After all, I loved to write and had my BA in English, so writing was something I was good at.

After a while, I was all set to apply. I had all of my documents, and my essay was finished. The only thing that bothered me was the high tuition. I knew I would have to take out loans. I took out a loan to finish my last semester at U of L, but my mother said she would pay that off, so I didn't have any experience with loans. With all of the fees at NYU, I would have to take out loans for about $70,000. I was scared that I wouldn't be able to pay it back. So as I was talking about the application process at work one day, I spoke to one of the doctors (I was working in a psychiatric hospital with children at the time) about my reservations, and he told me that he felt the same way when he was applying to medical school. He told me the same advice that he was told: "Don't let money get in the way of your decision." So I went home, gathered my documents, prayed, asked God to let me get into NYU if that is where He wanted me to be, and mailed my application. For the next eight weeks, all I could do was anxiously await a reply.

Since I had my hopes set on moving to New York and going to NYU, I began working a part-time job as a substitute teacher, and I also moved in with my grandma. It was during this time of me waiting and saving money that I awoke to one of the biggest shocks of my life: I couldn't move my hands!

There was nothing special about the day before my life changed forever. So imagine my surprise when I woke up in the morning and couldn't move my hands. My fingers and hands were cramped so badly it was painful. My hands were formed as if I had two mitts on and was waiting to catch two softballs. At first, I didn't know what to do. I went to my grandmother and showed her my hands. On her advice to go to the emergency room, I got dressed and went to the University of Louisville Hospital right away. I don't remember how I managed to drive there, but I did. (I've always been pretty independent, to a fault sometimes!) I waited in the emergency room until I was called, and when the doctor looked at my hands, he told me I had carpal tunnel.

He couldn't tell me why I was having an onset of carpal tunnel, which concerned me because I had always been relatively healthy. However, he did tell me to start wearing a brace to stabilize my right wrist. Now, I woke up in the morning with both wrists cramped. But by the time I was seen in the emergency room, my hands were beginning to relax, so I received only one brace because my right wrist was worse off than my left. The doctor explained I wouldn't have to wear it all the time, only when my wrist started cramping up. I thanked him, was discharged, and went home to tell my grandmother what happened. She agreed with the diagnosis, and that made me feel better. I wasn't used to having something wrong with me. Since my grandmother knew about carpal tunnel syndrome, I felt better knowing she agreed with the doctor.

Throughout my remaining time in Louisville, both of my wrists would take turns cramping up. One day I would have to wear the brace on my left wrist to help it relax, which meant I was overcompensating with my right hand. Then the next morning, I would have to put the brace on my right wrist and wear it all day, which meant I would overcompensate with my left hand. The cramping became so consistent I had to go out and buy another brace. At this point, I was becoming irritated because, other than wearing the brace, I didn't have any other medical advice to help me cope with the carpal tunnel, and my condition wasn't improving. When my hands began to cramp, I would feel tingling in my palms and fingertips, and sometimes my fingers would swell. My fingertips would also turn blue.

I'm not exactly sure when, but at one point, I realized putting on and removing braces for the rest of my life wasn't what I wanted.

Since I had no other options from the hospital, I began to look online to see if I could pinpoint what was happening with my hands and the changing symptoms. This wasn't the first time I felt like I needed answers. As a matter of fact, needing to know everything was what I was known for in my family. My mom used to call me "the nose knows," and she would say, "If anybody knows, the nose knows!" Even though I didn't like the nickname, it described me well.

It was during this time of frustration that I first heard about lupus. The more I looked at the symptoms of systemic lupus erythematosus (SLE), the more I was convinced I had it. Since I would be leaving in less than a month, I decided to wait until I got to NYU to talk to the doctors about whether or not I had lupus.

As I walked into the apartment after work one day, my grandmother let me know a package had come for me, and she had put it on the dining room table. I walked over to the table, put my purse and keys down, and looked at my mail. It was from NYU! I nervously opened the package, and the first thing I saw on the first sheet of paper was, "Congratulations!" I immediately turned to my grandmother and told her I got in. Then I called my mother and sisters to tell them the good news. My older sister said she would work on getting us an apartment. (After hearing I would be in New York for school, she enrolled at a school in New York as well so we could be together.) My mother said she would fly and meet me in New York so she could go with me to orientation and help me move into the new apartment. Things were coming together!

On my last day working for Norton Hospital in the psychiatry wing, my coworkers wished me well and gave me going away presents. I was sad to leave because I had great coworkers, but I was excited to be going to school to continue my education. One of my coworkers had always admired my African scrubs, so I gave them to her on my last day with the rest of my scrubs. She was thrilled! I also made sure I said goodbye to all the kids I worked with. Most of them colored pictures for me and told me they would miss me.

I was excited and nervous when I left Louisville for New York, but since I knew NYU was the place God wanted me to be, I also felt confident. My mom's best friend, Glenna, picked me up from the airport and took me to the apartment my sister had found for the two of us in Brooklyn.

We lived in a Brownstone building in the second-floor apartment. A single mother and her two kids lived in the first-floor apartment, and the landlords lived in the basement. Our apartment was small. It was a railroad apartment. Once you entered, you walked right into the kitchen. To the left of the kitchen were the rest of the rooms in a straight line. First came the living room (the bathroom sat to the side in the living room), then my room, then my sister's room. So to reach my sister's room, you had to walk through my room. I didn't mind too much. The rent wasn't expensive, and I liked the hardwood floors. That first day I remember thinking how different New York was from Kentucky and how fun it would be living with Melissa. We went to the grocery store and unpacked boxes. It was hard work that first day, but I was excited to be there. However, we had some problems right from the beginning.

My first night in the apartment was spent on a blow-up mattress on the floor because I didn't have any furniture. My mom was coming into town to buy furniture and help me. My TV was on the floor beside my mattress, playing a movie, and I watched the movie until I fell asleep. I woke up in the middle of the night and saw a mouse enter my room from the kitchen and proceed through my room into my sister's room. I was shocked to see the mouse, but I wasn't scared. I just remained still, and it didn't seem to notice me. I thought if we kept the apartment clean, it would eventually go away, but I was wrong. I saw it during the night a few more times after that. When I no longer saw it scurrying to and fro on the floor, I saw evidence that it was still around.

My sister used to leave the bread on the counter. One morning we woke up, and the mouse had gotten into the bread. Its teeth marks were visible in the loaf. So we started putting all of the food in the fridge. Well, that solved the problem of the mouse getting into our food, but it didn't stop bugs from crawling into the cabinets. I remember opening the cabinet for some seasonings, and bugs were crawling all over them! Now that did freak me out! Melissa told the landlords, but nothing happened. She started getting into heated conversations with them because we didn't feel we should have to pay rent if our apartment was unlivable.

When my mom came into town, she didn't like the apartment that we were staying in or the neighborhood. Melissa told Mom about everything and explained she didn't think we'd be there much longer because of the conditions.

After my mom and I went furniture shopping, we went to campus. On the way, she told me about the trains and how to read the maps so I would know where I was going and what side of the platform I needed to stand on. I am directionally challenged, and I'm always getting lost, so my mother wanted to explain things since she used to live in New York and didn't want me to ask strangers many questions. Another thing my mother told me was that I wasn't supposed to stare at people and shouldn't make eye contact with anyone on the train. My mother explained sometimes people might take it the wrong way.

Once we arrived on campus, I went to orientation and met my academic advisor. It was a lot of walking! My legs hurt by the time I returned home, and so did my feet since I had unwisely put on slide-in sandals. Nonetheless, I was wiser because I knew more about NYU and when my insurance would start. I was still having problems with my hands, but I was becoming used to them, so it wasn't as much of a shock anymore. However, I still wanted a second opinion and knew I would get a good one at the NYU Student Health Center. I was glad school was starting soon because the stress of my sister and the landlords arguing about the condition of our apartment was wearing on me.

After one such argument, we were awakened early the next morning by banging on our door. Melissa went to see who it was and found the brother of one of our landlords. His sister had let him in the building, and he began threatening my sister and me, telling us we better have his sister's rent by the end of the day. Well, first, the last day for us to pay rent hadn't even passed, so our rent wasn't late and second, he had no right threatening us and telling us he would be back. So we did the only logical thing we could think of: we called the police.

Once the officers arrived, they allowed us to gather our belongings and move. One of the officers stayed with us during the process, and the other officer stayed with the landlords. While the police were there, we found out that the night before, while we were upstairs, the tenant on the first floor and the landlords got into a physical altercation, of which the first-floor tenant won. This was why the landlord's brother was so upset when he was threatening me and my sister. The police told the landlords they had no right to allow someone into the building. When they began to tell him that we hadn't paid our rent, he told them they would have to take us to court. My sister and I called Glenna. She came and picked us up and let us move into her old apartment in Manhattan that same day. Glenna was actually looking for tenants, and my sister and I needed a place to stay, so things worked out for all of us!

The apartment was wonderful! Not only was it located right off the A C line, but it was also right across from Central Park, and the apartment had been remodeled. We had granite countertops, stainless steel appliances and, best of all, no mice! Our old landlords did sue Melissa. However, since their brownstone was located in a two-family zoning area, which meant they were only allowed to have two families living in the building, and they had three families living in the building (including themselves), they lost!

The day my insurance started, I walked into the NYU Student Health Center and asked to be seen by their best doctor. I was told Dr. Turnoff was the doctor in charge and I asked if I could meet with him that day. When my name was called, I entered one of the examination rooms, where I met Dr. Turnoff. I explained to him that I had lupus. Now I was pretty sure of myself during that conversation. I had done the research. I had kept track of my changing symptoms. Of course, I knew what I had. I'm the nose!

However, like any good doctor, he listened, had labs drawn, and told me what he thought could be happening with my body. He told me the results from my labs would take a few days. When he called to update me on the results, he told me I had rheumatoid arthritis. He explained the symptoms of lupus and rheumatoid arthritis, RA, were similar and suggested I start seeing a rheumatologist. He referred me to a doctor off campus and told me to come back and see him anytime.

CHAPTER 2: BITTERSWEET

The minute I started going to Dr. Sara B. Kramer, I knew I liked her. She was the first doctor I started seeing regularly for RA. She was patient, kind, didn't mind answering my questions, and did a great job explaining her answers so that I understood what she was saying. Within my first few visits, she prescribed me medications for RA. The main drug I began taking was methotrexate. I was glad to have the medication because I was told it would make the symptoms in my hands go away. But it was a challenge for me. My first few tries took longer than expected because I couldn't swallow the pills (some were big). After all, it wasn't part of my normal routine. Then, I would sometimes forget to take my medication. However, after my body became used to swallowing the pills and I started feeling the benefits of taking the medication, I did a better job taking my meds as scheduled.

For the first two months, things were great. I was taking my medications, and my symptoms were under control. My classes were great, and I liked my professors. I was also making new friends. Bertina (B), Kirstin, Gary, Nicole, and I enjoyed many adventures together. We tried new ethnic restaurants almost every week, explored the city, and studied for our tests together.

Me and Nicole!

Me and Kirsten!

Me, Gary, and Nicole!

Me and B!

When the five of us weren't together, B and I were because we had the same classes. We shopped, ate, and prayed together. We had a lot in common and became close friends! I encouraged B when she confided in me her call to ministry and wasn't sure what her family would say since they weren't Christians. B encouraged me and looked out for me on the days I didn't feel well when I was struggling with being sick. We took care of one another.

We used to go to a lounge by NYU on the weekends when we had time. The house band was a group of six or seven attractive men of all races who could sing and play instruments. They were awesome. B and I would sit in one of the booths to the left of the stage and listen to the music or dance on the dance floor. We went so often that some band members began to recognize us. In between sets, they would come and talk to us. During the sets, they would even sing to us. However, it was all in good fun. They knew we weren't interested in anything more than friendship, so they knew if they sang to us, we wouldn't take it the wrong way. However, there were a lot of ladies who always scowled at me and B because we always seemed to have the band's attention. Still, we didn't mind. We loved the atmosphere and went often.

I was also enjoying spending time with my sister Melissa. We hadn't lived together since we were both in high school, and since she lived in DC, it was hard for me to visit her as often as I wanted. So it was good to see her every day and hang out with her. She explained that since I lived in the city, I would need a device to listen to music. So right before school started, I went with her and purchased my first Apple product, a green iPod. She had to show me how to put music on it since I've never been good with electronics. That's just one of my many fond memories of living with my sister.

New York itself was better than I expected. You hear stories of northerners and how they don't speak to you, and my mom told me not to look anyone in the eye, so I thought folks wouldn't be that friendly. However, they were! Anytime I asked someone for directions, they helped me, and the two times I fell really hard outside (once in a big puddle of water), a man would always ask me if I was all right and help me to my feet (yes, I am totally a clutz)!

Besides the people being friendly, I liked having many things to do. Just walking down the street could turn into an adventure because you never knew what you would see, hear and smell. You had vendors selling bags, clothes, music, perfume, and more. You had artists playing on corners and food trucks selling food that smelled wonderful. It seemed there was something different on every corner. I've always had this fascination with Asia, so I took many trips to China Town to eat the food and see the people. The ethnic food in New York tasted much better than what I was used to eating in Kentucky. So I definitely tried to walk when I could so I wouldn't miss anything!

When I wasn't wandering around the city (sometimes getting lost), I went to off-Broadway plays for free because we would get students tickets. And anyone who knows me well knows I like free things! I also made time to volunteer by working with the America Reads/America Counts program, which helped students become proficient in reading and math.

I was also acclimating myself to my new campus. NYU has a huge campus, but since I was in the Steinhardt School of Education, I didn't have far to walk between classes. My classes were challenging at first. I started off taking courses in psychology, but they were taught as if I had a background in psych, and I didn't. My background was in English, and I had only taken one psychology class, so things were stressful. In my theory course, I remember learning about all the different theories and struggling because it was all new information and a lot of it. I went to my professor for help, but that didn't end up being fruitful, so B helped me. Her undergraduate degree was in psychology, so this information wasn't new to her. I ended up passing the course with a B. However, because of all the stress, I ended up popping a blood vessel in my eye!

So life was good! My grades were awesome. I had new friends (of all different races), and my body felt like it was back to normal.

Toward the end of November and the beginning of December 2006, I began to be in constant pain. The pain moved from my hands to the rest of my body. It wasn't like a stinging pain or acute pain. It was like a migraine that wouldn't go away, like a paralyzing pain. And to make matters worse, the cold weather stiffened my body, and I had trouble walking and moving. There were days when I literally looked like a zombie walking with outstretched arms because the stiffness was so intense my arms wouldn't lay at my sides. I started taking Tylenol to help with the pain, but as my symptoms progressed and the pain became stronger, the Tylenol no longer worked. Until now, I was handling the stiffness in my wrists and hands with a positive, optimistic attitude. However, when the pain and stiffness spread all over my body, it became much harder for me to remain positive. I became depressed, thinking things would never return to normal and I would have to be in pain for the rest of my life.

Even though I was in constant pain, I still had to wake up, go to class and work. During my group dynamics class, I remember talking about how hard it was to stay on top of my studies while having health complications. One of my classmates said that I should just stop school and focus on getting better. I told him I didn't come all this way to give up or flunk out. That was the truth. My education has always been important, and I was determined to persevere. My classmate thought I was making things harder for myself than they needed to be. However, I knew one of my goals was to finish school on schedule, and I wouldn't let anything, including my health, deter me from that. Things were hard but not impossible, so I had to keep going.

It wasn't just the pain and stiffness. My medications were making me lethargic, and I started falling asleep in class. I was so tired all of the time. It was hard for me to keep my head up. So because of the pain, when I didn't have to be around others, I just stayed in my room. I tried to rest a lot, stay warm and do as little as possible because everything hurt. I stopped hanging out with friends and exploring the city. Even though I didn't tell anyone how bad I really felt, my friends and Melissa could tell by looking at me and the way I moved that I was in pain. There were days that I didn't have any energy at all and slept most of the day. On other days I couldn't lift items and struggled to drink because I couldn't lift the cup to my mouth. Life was an endless cycle of pain, and I was miserable.

I did still speak to family and friends on the phone. Most of them didn't know what I was going through at the time because I ensured my voice sounded upbeat. I didn't want them to worry because they weren't in New York and couldn't really help me.

With the pain and tiredness, I wasn't eating as much, so I started losing weight. It was hard for me to concentrate on eating because the pain was so overwhelming. Most days, I tried to get relief by being still. However, that didn't work. Getting more sleep didn't work. Using an ice pack or a heating pad didn't work. Everything hurt, and I wasn't finding any relief from the pain.

I was in my room one night thinking about the pain. At this point, I had been in constant pain all over for about three months. It hurt to sit, to stand, to blink, to move. It hurt to talk, to breathe. It hurt to be alive. So I began praying, telling God that I couldn't take the pain any longer and that if I had to live the rest of my life like this, He could just take me now (I have a bit of the dramatic flair). After I prayed, I went over to my medications and began reading the labels. One of my medications helped with the pain. Even though I was supposed to take only one and had already taken one earlier in the day, I remember thinking what would happen if I took another one. Now, I knew I wouldn't die from taking two (I had just read the label), but I didn't know exactly what would happen if I doubled my dose. I hesitated before I took it because I didn't want to make things worse for myself. Ultimately, I was so desperate for the pain to go away that the consequence that came really didn't matter. I took the pill, and all my pain vanished within an hour! My body was back to normal. I could breathe, sit, walk, talk, and do everything without pain. It was truly unbelievable! It felt like I was in a new body. I had been in pain for so long that I forgot how it felt to be normal. And I also didn't experience any ill side effects from doubling the medication, so I began taking two every day instead of one to keep the pain at bay.

I did this for about a week before I was able to see Dr. Kramer. When I told her what I had been doing, she looked alarmed. She told me taking such a high dose of that medication could affect my kidneys and ordered me to stop. However, with that command, she prescribed another medication to help with the pain. And it never returned!

Things started returning to normal in my life. I was so grateful to have another chance at life without pain. Just moving my body made things seem so surreal because I never imagined I would be able to walk and talk again without pain. I still had stiffness at night and in cold weather, but the constant pain was gone. I began hanging out with friends again and shopping. I thought the worst of things was over.

One day shortly after, I began to have pain when I breathed. This started happening while I was on campus, so I went to see Dr. Turnoff. When I mentioned it to him, he took X-rays of my chest and informed me I had fluid in my lungs. He told me that fluid in the lungs was a symptom of lupus and that sometimes the fluid went away on its own. He said if it didn't go away, I would have to have it removed. Well, it didn't go away. So, on January 7, 2007, I had my first procedure on my left lung. I was nervous. I was glad I didn't have to have anesthesia or stay overnight in the hospital. It was still frightening, though. Before the fluid could be removed, I saw a pulmonologist (fancy word for lung doctor) at the hospital, and he took X-rays of my lungs to see exactly where the fluid in my left lung was. He was very friendly and stayed with me during the procedure, holding my hand and explaining everything that was happening. After he explained a step, the person performing the procedure would carry it out. So there were no surprises, and I liked that because I needed to know what to expect to help with my anxiety about the situation.

I had to remove my shirt and bra and put on a hospital gown with an opening at the back. They had me lean over a padded bench and told me to relax. The first thing they did was numb my back. The pulmonologist told me I could squeeze his hand once I felt the needle prick if I wanted. I did. The second thing they did was insert a long needle into my back to extract the fluid. Did I mention how long the needle was? It was really long! They removed most of the fluid and showed me the fluid in the needle when the procedure was over. I remember it looking similar to chicken broth. They took another X-ray of my lungs and, satisfied with what they saw, sent me home.

I had a follow-up appointment with the pulmonologist and with Dr. Kramer. She also mentioned that fluid in the lungs was a symptom of systemic lupus erythematosus (SLE), and she ran more tests on me. However, when they returned, they still showed I was positive for rheumatoid arthritis and negative for SLE. So, needless to say, I was confused, and my doctor was a little puzzled as well. Still, she continued to monitor me closely.

On February 6, 2007, Dr. Kramer noticed small bumps on my neck and armpits. She told me they were lymph nodes, which could be cancerous. She set up an appointment for me at the NYU Cancer Institute. The doctor that saw me told me he needed to take samples for testing. To do this, a needle was stuck in the lymph nodes to extract fluid. The doctor said it would take a week before the results came back. I remember that being one of the longest weeks of my life! I knew something more than RA was happening inside my body, but I didn't want it to be cancer! Cancer just sounded so final in my mind. Waiting for those results was hard on my family as well. My mother constantly worried about me, and so did my sisters and friends. A week later, when I received the call from the Cancer Institute with my results, I was in my evening group dynamics class. I stepped outside into the hall, answered my phone, and heard the best news of my life up until that point. The lymph nodes weren't cancerous! I was so relieved. I called my mom immediately to let her know the good news. She was happy for me and told the rest of the family. I also went inside and told my classmates, and they were happy for me as well. Still, it wasn't until March 2007 that I heard the news I will never forget.

"You have lupus."

It was sunny outside. As the doctor told me my diagnosis, I stopped walking and listened. I smiled as I felt a sense of relief because what was happening to me finally had a name. At the time, I thought it was something I would be able to manage. I believed things would only go up from here. Dr. Kramer told me she would change my medications, and she began telling me other things that I would now have to be mindful of with my new diagnosis. One of those things was I needed to avoid sun exposure, more specifically, ultraviolet rays.

Ultraviolet rays, UV, can cause UV photosensitivity in individuals with lupus. This means individuals exposed to UV rays can experience symptoms of feeling sick, joint pain, chills, etc. Dr. Kramer told me I needed to try to do all of my errands before the sun rose and after the sun set. She also said I had to start wearing sunscreen every day. Avoiding UV rays was tough for me for two reasons. The first was my classes were all in the afternoon, so I had to walk back and forth on campus in the sun. The second was I loved being outside in the sun and feeling the sun on my skin. So it was tough. At times, I forgot to wear sunscreen. On those days, when the sun's rays hit my skin, I would physically feel sick. Once that happened a few times, I didn't forget to wear my sunscreen and hat any longer, and I did my best to stay out of the sun when it was its brightest and did all of my errands in the evening. However, March turned out the be bittersweet in the end. Even though I had a name for what was happening in my body, I had no idea a storm was brewing ahead.

CHAPTER 3:
GRATEFUL FOR PAJAMAS

On April 12, 2007, I woke up and didn't feel well. I hadn't ever felt this way before, so I wasn't sure what to do. It was hard for me to take deep breaths, and I felt sharp pains in the sides of my stomach. Still, being the type of person I am, I tried not to concentrate on how I felt and went to class and tried to make the best of things. However, as I was eating dinner with B before our last class of the day, I started to feel worse. And as we were walking back to class, I started not to be able to breathe. I could only take in a little air before I felt a sharp pain on my side. I began to panic and started crying. I called my rheumatologist and told her I couldn't breathe, and she told me to go straight away to see my doctor on campus.

I was right up the street from the NYU Medical Center, so it didn't take B and me long to get there. I walked in just as Dr. Turnoff was leaving. He took one look at me and had me accompany him to the back, where I told him about my symptoms. He took some X-rays, showed me cloudy pictures of my lungs with fluid in them, and told me I needed to go to the hospital right away. He told me to take my X-rays.

When I left his office, I told B what was happening and asked her to tell our professor why I wouldn't be in the class that evening. She hugged me and told me she would tell our professor. I went outside, hailed a cab to the hospital, and walked into the emergency room. Once I explained what was happening and showed one of the nurses the X-rays, I was moved to another section of the emergency room and given a bed. It didn't take long for a doctor to see me. He told me that I would be admitted that night because I would have to have surgery on my lung due to the fluid. I called my sister to let her know what was happening, and she told me she would call Mom and bring me an overnight bag and some snacks.

When Melissa arrived at the hospital, I was still in the emergency room area. It felt good to be lying down, and I was grateful for the bag and the snacks because I didn't finish my dinner earlier, and I was hungry. Melissa stayed with me until I was moved into my new room and given two gowns to put on. I wanted to keep my own clothes on, but when the nurse came in to insert my IV and saw my clothes, she said I wouldn't be able to wear them because they would prevent the doctors from getting to me the way they needed to. So I put on both gowns, one backward and the other the right way, so that my whole body was covered. Melissa didn't pack any pajamas in the bag because I didn't have any at home.

I've never been a big fan of pajamas. It's always a chore trying to find pajamas that fit me in all the right places. I'm tall, and when I look for bottoms, they're all too short. So I have to end up getting pajamas a size bigger than I need to get the length, but then they don't fit well. So I decided to just stop buying them and wear shorts and a T-shirt to bed.

However, after the nurse explained that I could put on a pajama top that buttoned down the front, Melissa told me she would buy some and bring them to me the next day. When visiting hours were over, Melissa asked me what else I wanted her to bring, told me she loved me and that she would be back tomorrow. She said she would call Mom and give her an update.

The next day Melissa returned with two pairs of pajamas for me. They were the kind I needed: a top that buttoned down the front and long pants. I'd never been so grateful for a pair of pj's! During my first evening in the hospital, I realized how cold it was, and I was delighted I had warm clothes to wear instead of hospital gowns!

Once my mom heard I would be having surgery, she took off work and came to New York to stay with me for the procedure. My surgeon, Dr. Crawford, was a nice, funny guy who talked to me so that I could understand and answered the questions my mom and I had. He was confident the surgery would be successful.

The day before my surgery, I met my anesthesiologist. He reviewed the paperwork with me and asked me to sign it, giving permission to receive anesthesia. After he left my room, I prayed and asked God to bless everyone involved in my surgery and the surgery itself. I slept soundly that night.

The next day, as I was being taken away for surgery, my mom became tearful and told me that she loved me. I reassured her that I would be fine. At that point, I was handling the surgery better than she was! However, that was my personality. I had already prayed, so I just tried to stay optimistic. Once I was in the operating room, Dr. Crawford held my hand as I was given the anesthesia. He talked to me and made me feel relaxed. The last thing I remember hearing is him asking me why a pretty girl like me didn't have a boyfriend.

When I opened my eyes, the surgery was over. I was told it went well and that the fluid in my left lung shouldn't ever return, and it hasn't! I had to take it easy after my surgery. I had a bandage on the left side of my back from the incision, and it was painful. I didn't take much pain medication because I only wanted to take it when I absolutely needed it. I also tried to do as many things on my own as I could. Even though my mom was there and offered to help me, I didn't want to depend on others to help me with things I could get accomplished on my own. So even if it took twice as long, I tried to do everything myself.

A few days after my surgery, an intern came into my room and told me she would remove the bandage from my back. She had me sit up and told me that it shouldn't hurt, so I didn't brace myself for any pain. She began to tear the bandage off quickly, and the pain was so intense that my eyes watered immediately. My mouth fell open, but no sound came out. She didn't have a good grasp on the bandage and ended up having to pull it twice before it came all the way off. It hurt really bad. I made a mental note never to believe that intern because she didn't tell the truth about the pain. My mom saw my face and told me that it wasn't a big deal and that it was over. So I willed my body to calm down. I had to go to the bathroom, so as I moved to get off the bed, my mom came to help me, but I told her I could do it myself. As I walked to the bathroom, which was about ten steps from my bed, I heard my mom tell the intern that I'd always been independent.

What my mother said was true, but life circumstances made me that way. For example, in middle school, I always used to ask my mom to curl my hair so I could wear it down. Well, she would say no more than I liked, so I finally decided to learn to do my hair so I wouldn't have to ask her. After some practice, I did my hair so well my mom started asking me to do certain styles on her hair as well! So, it was situations like this that made me learn to depend on myself.

On one of the days I was in the hospital, I was about to eat my meal when a lady came into my room and asked to speak with me. She said she was a dietician. Now, I had lost some weight because I hadn't been feeling well, and she was concerned about that. She told me that I needed to get my weight up, and my mom and I both reassured her that I love to eat. I explained to her that when I don't feel well and have constant pain, my mind doesn't think of anything but the pain, so I forget to eat, which is why I had lost so much weight. She had me look at a menu to pick out my meals for the upcoming days and told me she would have the people in charge of meals put extra snacks on my plate since she wanted to try to put some weight on me before I left the hospital. I was happy about the extra food, but my happiness was short-lived once I saw what my "extra snacks" were. They were Boost drinks! Yuck! Here I had my hopes set on some pop tarts or chips or yogurt, and I received a chalky-tasting drink! Boost is used for meal substitution, and it's packed with protein but not a good flavor! Needless to say, I didn't care for them, but I did drink them since I knew that's what my dietician wanted me to do.

While in the hospital, B came to visit me and brought me some of my favorite snacks (yep, talking about food again) and some card games that we played together. Randy, my good friend and one of the personal trainers from the gym, came to sit with me as well and brought me some snacks. Since Randy is all about eating healthy, he brought me some fresh fruit!

Randy and I became close friends when I started working at the gym. I loved exercising and decided that I wanted to be a personal trainer. Randy was already a successful trainer as well as a model, and we cliqued instantly! When he didn't have clients, we would always hang out at the gym. He would give me some great workout routines, and he taught me how to be a healthier eater. He even let me sit in some of his workout sessions with his clients so I could learn more about personal training. When I was around Randy, I always ate super healthy. Moreover, Randy was my one friend that always got on me for slouching. He would always tell me how bad it was for my posture and would tell me to sit up if I was slouching. To this day, sometimes I catch myself when I'm slouching, and I'll sit up because I'm reminded of him.

Before being released from the hospital, I was given an antibiotic to take, and I received permission to fly out of town for spring break. I was excited about that because I needed a break, and since I had already paid for my tickets, I didn't want to waste my money. I didn't do anything too exciting. It was just an opportunity to hang out with people I cared about and relax after my ordeal. After being out of town that week, my body felt normal. Today, all that's left of that first surgery is the scar on my back.

After spring break, I tried to return to work at the gym, but it was hard because I couldn't lift more than five pounds. At that point, my goal of becoming a personal trainer was put on hold, and I had to find something to do that was more on my new level. So I began working at the gym's front desk. I was glad to still be in the environment, be around my friends, and still have a job to work, even though the front desk didn't pay that well. However, a few months after my surgery, the pain in my body began to return, and I started to feel poorly again.

One night as I was talking to another young lady who worked the front with me, she could tell that I didn't feel well. I told her I had lupus and shared with her some of the things I was struggling with. She told me that the only person she ever knew with lupus had died. She gave me what I would call a pity look. I told her that I didn't want to resign from my position at the gym, but working full time and always having to stand while at work was too much for me right now. I remember telling her that I just didn't want to disappoint or let anyone down by resigning. She said the gym would be fine whether I was there or not and that I needed to take care of myself and my health. After our conversation, I thought about what she said and decided to find another job. Randy and I still stayed in touch, though, and sometimes I would babysit his daughter for him!

So in July 2007, I began working at an arts camp with kids. It was great because I returned to one of my first loves: working with children. Some had singing lessons, while others played musical instruments or took art classes. We went on field trips to the zoo, Madame Toussan's Wax Museum, and many other exciting places. We even recorded our own CD of the kids singing the songs the camp counselors taught them over the months of camp. I could sit a lot while working at the camp, which allowed me to enjoy walking and exploring with the kids. I also had many opportunities to be outside, and since I didn't feel sick anymore due to the sun, I was happy. Whether inside or out in the sun, I loved the job and was glad for the extra money because I had received the bill from the hospital, and the surgery and hospital stay added up to over $5,000. I was a little worried about how I would pay it off.

However, even though the hospital bill was in the back of my mind, I didn't worry about it that much because I had been told there was a fund for NYU students that helped pay their medical bills. So when I started to worry about my bills, I just prayed, reminded myself that when classes resumed, I would look into the medical relief fund, and I just kept moving forward.

Even though I no longer worried about fluid building up in my lungs, I still had days when I felt lethargic and had low energy. On July 14, 2007, I couldn't walk because of the pain and swelling in my joints. On the 17th of that month, I started developing ulcers in my mouth. One thing I can tell you that I learned early on was to try to enjoy myself when I was down because I knew there wasn't anything I could do about it. When I needed to rest, I just started watching more TV.

On August 4, 2007, I woke up to prepare for work at the arts camp and didn't feel well. It wasn't the same feeling I had felt with my lungs. It was different. However, being the trooper that I am, I pushed through the pain, dressed, and went to work. Upon arriving, I still didn't feel well. The kids were going on a field trip that day and were excited. I was sitting with my group, and I kept feeling worse. I went to the bathroom, broke out in a cold sweat, and became very dizzy. I knew I needed to go home. I could barely stand, my heart was beating erratically, and my vision was blurred. I walked slowly back to my group, told Jason, one of the camp leaders, that I was going home and started to gather my belongings. After Jason looked at me, he went to get the director. As I was sitting down, she came up to me and saw that something was wrong and asked me what the matter was. I told her I didn't know. She told me she was uncomfortable letting me catch the bus home and called for a cab. Even though I didn't have any money, the cab driver took me home, and once there, my sister paid him and helped me inside.

I called the hospital and told the woman who answered I didn't feel well. I explained that I had lupus and told her some symptoms I had experienced that morning. She then asked if I had a temperature. I did. She said that even though I had a temperature, it wasn't dangerously high and told me to take some aspirin and wait an hour. Now, I don't want you to think she wasn't doing her job well. With lupus, when you don't feel well, it's hard to tell at first if you don't feel well because of lupus or because you have a cold or something more common. So you have to take medication to see if that helps your symptoms. If it does, then you know it's not the lupus.

She said if my fever didn't go down or worsened, I would need to come in right away. So I took some medicine and went to sleep. When I woke up that evening, my fever was 104, so I called my doctor's office and was told to go straight to the hospital. I told my sister where I was going and called for a cab. Once the nurse saw how high my temperature was and heard some of my symptoms, I was taken to have X-rays of my chest. The X-rays revealed fluid in my heart sac. I was told the fluid was restricting the movement of my heart. I was admitted that night because I needed to have another surgery.

Once again, my mom came and stayed with me while I was in the hospital. My sister brought my things for me. Before my surgery, I remember feeling my heart beat erratically. Sometimes it would beat really fast, and other times it would beat slowly. The rapid changes scared me. I was also scared because this experience was different from the first time I was in the hospital, so I didn't know what to expect. And that's one of the things I don't like about lupus it always looks different.

I also couldn't go into surgery as early as the doctors wanted because I was anemic and needed a blood transfusion before they would operate. The transfusion was painless. I remember seeing the blood in a bag and going through an IV into my body. I remember being given two bags of blood. Once the doctors dealt with the anemia, they scheduled me for surgery.

I don't remember everything that happened while I was in the hospital the second time, just some bits and pieces. I remember being woken up in the morning to have my blood drawn. Up until that point, I didn't have any problem with needles. However, during my stay, I had to have labs drawn two or three times a day, and some of the people didn't do a good job. I remember being stuck three times by a woman because she kept missing my vein. Even Dr. Kramer had to stick me more than once because my veins kept moving. I grew to dread having my blood drawn.

One morning as I was woken up to have my labs drawn, I was talking to the gentleman about the horrors I had endured while people poked me to draw blood. As he was putting his gloves on, he told me that I had nothing to worry about with him because he was the best at drawing blood. Then he smiled at me, and that put me at ease. As he took the needle into his hand, I braced myself for pain since that was what I was used to. However, he told me I could relax, felt my arm, quickly inserted the needle, and I felt no pain. He asked me if I had felt anything, and I said no. He smiled, and I thanked him for doing a good job. The lupus and the way it was affecting my body were out of my control, but being appreciative of the small things wasn't. I always continued to try and see the bright side. And I seemed to do a good job because my friends told me later the one thing they remembered about me was I always smiled.

Another thing I remember about being in the hospital the second time is one morning, a team of interns came in with the doctor to learn about my case. I remember feeling like a lab experiment. If they could have oohed and aahed, I'm sure they would have. Now mind you, I was in pain, waiting for this surgery to take place, and I had all these students coming in every morning wanting to ask me questions, get a look at me, and take turns using their stethoscopes on me. It was exasperating.

Not only that, but I also had a kidney biopsy during my stay in the hospital. I was continually hounded to be in an upcoming study for lupus patients. Now I know lupus research is important, but I just wasn't in the mood. It was draining enough to try to remain positive with the things happening with my body as it was. I didn't want to add any extra stress on myself.

I was glad to find out Dr. Crawford would be my surgeon again. I was also glad my rheumatologist, Dr. Kramer, came to see me and discussed my care with the doctor over my case in the hospital. I remember hearing her give my hospital doctor orders that he willingly followed. So I knew I was in good hands. Dr. Crawford explained that to get to my heart sac, he would cut me under my left breast, not to leave any unnecessary visible scars, and insert a tube so that the fluid could drain out on its own. He said when I woke up, I would have the tube in my chest and that it would have to stay there until it was completely dry. This meant I would have to lay flat in bed without moving for as long as it took.

I was more nervous about this surgery than the first one because they were operating on my heart sac. This surgery took longer than the surgery on my lungs, and both my sister and my mom stayed in the waiting room during my surgery. After my surgery, they came to see me in the recovery room. I remember them talking to me, but I cannot remember what was said because I was very groggy from the anesthesia. I do remember telling them that I love them, and once they left, I fell asleep. When I opened my eyes, I was in the intensive care unit.

I stayed in the ICU for two days. I was allowed to have a TV, so my sister brought my favorite DVDs to the hospital for me. At that time, I was an avid fan of Grey's Anatomy, but I couldn't bring myself to watch it while in the hospital. Actually, I don't remember watching a lot of TV. What I do remember is wearing a catheter with a bladder bag and being told all of my snacks had been thrown away because they could only keep them for a couple of days (they knew they were wrong) in the hospital. I also remember being the healthiest person in ICU. From my bed, I could see some of the other patients who were old and looked like they were about to die. I had no visitors during my stay in ICU. It was a little depressing. The nurses working on their different shifts didn't spend any time talking to me to see how I was because the other patients needed their attention more than I did.

I remember laying on my back and looking at the tube coming out of my chest and the fluid going down the tube. I didn't know how long I would be stuck in my bed. I knew I looked like a hot mess, unable to brush my teeth or wash my face or shower. It was tough. I had to stay as still as possible so as not to disturb the tube. All I thought about was my life and how I wanted things to be when I was released (yep, it felt like prison). I was on a fluid diet, so I always felt hungry. I questioned God because I couldn't understand why He would choose to make me sick and prohibit me from reaching my dreams. I didn't understand why I had to be sick while away from my family and friends. I was becoming stressed because I was missing class, and I felt bad because everyone constantly worried about me. Still, there was nothing I could do about any of it. I just had to lie there.

In the evening, on my second day in the ICU, one of the nurses came over to check my tube and saw that it was completely dry. She told me she would remove the tube, and I would be moved to a hospital room. I was excited to be able to move but became nervous because I began to think about the last surgery and how the intern removed the bandage and said it wouldn't hurt when it ended up hurting really bad. As the nurse returned to check on me, she noticed that my heart monitor showed my pulse was elevated. She asked me what was wrong, and I tearfully told her. She said she was sorry I didn't get much attention while I was in the ICU and reassured me as she stroked my head that it wouldn't hurt. I know it sounds silly, but in my head, I didn't want her to pull it out because I didn't want to go through that pain again. However, she put on gloves, told me to be still, and pulled the tube out, and I felt nothing. She put a bandage on me and said I would be moving soon. As I turned to lie on my side, I felt so relieved and glad to be moving to a regular room so I could have visitors again. I also felt delighted to be able to move and not have to be flat on my back.

In about an hour, I was moved to my new room, and my sister came to see me. After the nurse removed the bladder bag, my sister helped me into the shower since I couldn't do it alone. As she helped me walk out of the shower toward the towel, she joked and told me I looked like one of the malnourished kids you see in the commercials because I was so thin. The comment didn't offend me. I knew it was true, and I was glad to be off the fluid diet so I could start doing something about it!

For a few days after the surgery, I was taken at least once a day to have an ultrasound of my heart to ensure the fluid wasn't back. I still wore the pajamas my sister purchased, and I also asked for heated blankets anytime I traveled outside of my room. Sometimes I had to wait over an hour for an ultrasound, so I wanted to stay as warm as possible.

Once my discharge was set for August 14, Dr. Kramer discussed my new medication with me, prednisolone. She informed me the steroid I had been taking since my first surgery wasn't working. She said I needed to be switched to another steroid in the same family and prescribed a high dose of it for me because my body was still recovering from surgery. She explained that once someone reaches a dose of 8mg or higher of this steroid, that person could potentially gain weight and have other unpleasant side effects. I was put on a dose of 24mg twice a day. Even though I was warned about the side effects, I didn't think they would be something I would have to worry about because I had never suffered any side effects from the medications I took before. So after I was discharged, I took my meds, rested and forgot all about the side effects of the steroids until I woke up one morning and didn't recognize the face that stared back at me.

Chapter 4: Cheesin'

I don't know about you, but I love taking pictures of the exciting places I go, the people I meet, the activities I do, and if there's money left over, I like to bring home a souvenir for myself and others. The pictures are a good reminder of the great time I had with friends and family.

In 2012 I took a trip to New Orleans with the Missions Ministry at my church to work on houses with Habitat for Humanity. We worked on two houses and met the women who would move into them. I didn't have much money, but that didn't stop me from having a good time. Since I couldn't afford to buy a souvenir to take with me, I decided to take pictures of the interesting and funny souvenirs I saw. I called the pictures my picturenirs.

Just like those pictures helped me remember a short experience I had in New Orleans, the pictures in this book hold memories from one of the worst times in my life. I'm grateful I have them because I tried my hardest not to pose in any. I didn't like what I saw daily, so I had no desire to take pictures of myself or be in the pictures others were taking. Moreover, during this time, I didn't even write. Writing, for me, is like breathing. Words are who I am, and I've always written down my experiences and kept journals. During this time, though, I wrote nothing which speaks volumes. I had no desire to share this experience with others, let alone remember it myself.

However, as I prepared to write this book, I saw quite a few pictures of myself during this time on my computer. I saw myself gaining weight, the rash on my face and the aftermath of cutting all my hair. Even though I still don't like what I see when I view the pictures, the one thing I recognized was my smile. It remained the same in all of them.

I smile a lot. I smile when I'm happy, excited, and even nervous. I'm just always smiling. And I have a wide, toothy grin that I broadcast to the world. One of the slang words for smiling I used growing up was "cheesin'." My sisters and I would say, "cheesin' from ear to ear" if we saw someone with a wide smile.

So as I looked at the pictures and focused on my smile, it allowed me to realize that even though I was going through a tough situation, I still tried my hardest to make the best of it by smiling. I believe the act of smiling got me through many of the unexpected changes that lupus brought my way. Continuing to try to stay optimistic was one of the things my friends remembered about me that they grew to admire.

That's my challenge to you, friends. Stay optimistic in life no matter what unexpected circumstances come your way. It's hard but not impossible. I don't look like what I've gone through, and sharing my pictures might bring hope to someone who is struggling with their diagnosis at this moment. So, whoever you are, wherever you are, these pictures are for you.

Me at Coney Island before becoming sick

Within a few days after being discharged from the hospital, I started having side effects due to the high level of steroids I was on. I remember waking up a couple of days after starting on the steroids, looking in the mirror as I prepared for the day, and noticing my face looked different. It was weird because I had never felt like my face was different. However, the more I looked at myself, the more I realized my face was chubbier than normal. At this point, was it a huge noticeable difference? No. Still, I could tell a change had occurred. I went to my sister's room and asked her to look at my face and tell me if she noticed anything. She said she didn't see anything and that I was just imagining it. However, I wasn't. As the days passed, my face continued to look rounder and fuller.

In September, I went to a fraternity party on a boat with my sister Melissa and one of our friends, Jezelle. The Alpha Phi Alpha fraternity was throwing the party, so I knew many handsome men would attend. I was looking forward to having a good time and getting dressed up so I could feel pretty. My face was a lot chubbier and was broken out in a rash, but I wouldn't let that stop me. I wore one of my favorite black dresses for the event and ensured my accessories and makeup looked nice. I ended up seeing a guy there I thought was cute. I hesitated to speak with him, but Jezelle told me I looked beautiful and encouraged me. So I did, and we ended up exchanging phone numbers! Nothing ever came of it, but I was pleased that even though I didn't look like my regular self, I still had guys interested in me.

Me and Melissa, Alpha Party

Jezelle and Me, Alpha Party

Just as I was starting to get used to the chubbiness of my face, my body began to pick up weight. Remember that comment my sister made about being able to see my ribs? Well, I was about 120 pounds at the time. On August 21, a week after being on my new medication, I weighed 138 pounds! By the time September rolled around, I had begun to struggle to fit into my clothing. The interesting thing about the weight gain was it started on my midsection. So at times, it looked like I was pregnant. You can see an example of this in the next picture. I couldn't button my jacket all the way down. You can also see my face is much rounder here than in the last picture and that the rash is gone.

Me visiting my nieces in Philly

The best thing about the weight gain was that my sister and friends were very supportive. No one treated me any differently because I looked different. I don't even remember my family or friends giving me surprised looks as I continued to change and look different every time they saw me. Actually, I received some compliments. I was told I looked prettier and healthier with my full face. It seemed every time I was feeling my lowest, God would allow someone to say a kind word to me to boost my spirit and encourage me to keep moving forward.

The weekend before my 25th birthday, Melissa, some of my friends, and I got together at our apartment to celebrate. I had on my birthday outfit and was feeling good about myself. We ate good food, played games, and I had an M&M yellow ice cream cake since yellow is one of my favorite colors. My sister put a few candles on the cake, everyone sang happy birthday, and then I was told to blow out the candles. So I blew, but none of the candles went out. My sister and friends encouraged me to keep blowing, and I did, being the gullible person I am. On one of the blows, the candles flickered out but then came back, and I knew something was up. At that point, my sister and friends busted out laughing and told me they were trick candles.

My 25th birthday party

Less than two weeks after my birthday, I weighed 151 pounds. I took the weight gain as an opportunity to go shopping. It didn't make sense for me to keep trying to squeeze myself into my clothes and always feel uncomfortable. I tried to buy clothes made of spandex because if the jeans or pants were too tight, they hurt my legs.

Before the surgeries, I was a size two. When I weighed my heaviest, I was a size ten and weighed 160 pounds. Even with new clothes, I felt like everything I put on was really tight. During this time, I didn't care much about looking fashionable. My main objective was to be comfortable.

Christmas in Maryland. Me holding two of my cousins.

All the weight gain made it hard for me to walk. I couldn't go up the stairs or walk for long periods without needing to take a break. I became winded more quickly, and my knees and feet would always ache. I felt bogged down by all the weight and wasn't as active because I had no energy to workout. I knew once the side effects wore off, I would be small again. However, I didn't know how long I would have to be heavy until that happened.

One night, as I was going home, I got on the subway with an ice cream cone from McDonald's, and there were people on the train looking at me. Now I knew the look. It was the same look I had given people eating fattening food who were overweight. However, when I was given this look, it really hurt my feelings. I remember not even wanting the ice cream afterward. No one who saw me realized the reflection they saw wasn't me. They didn't know I was struggling with being sick and had gained weight due to my medications. They didn't know the weight gain wasn't my fault. All they saw was a chubby woman eating ice cream.

And it didn't help things when people close to me would tell me if I didn't like the way I looked, I should workout. Now they meant well. I'm sure if you had a friend who had gained weight and they complained about being bigger, you would tell them to workout too. However, what they didn't fully understand was lowering my dose of mediation would be the only way I could lose weight. That wouldn't happen anytime soon because my body needed steroids to function properly. So, for the time being, I was a skinny person stuck in a big body and no longer liked looking at myself in the mirror.

By the end of February 2008, my doctor decided I could start to lower my dose of steroids because my body was healing and functioning better. That was good news to my ears! I was ready to get my body back and become more active. I missed working out and being able to walk around the city with ease. I still felt joint pain and stiffness daily, especially in my chest and hands. However, since the pain wasn't as bad as before, and I was recovering my body, I didn't dwell on it too much.

Me and Aisha!

By March, my face was looking more like my old self. It felt so good to look in the mirror every morning and see the little changes that allowed me to see more of myself. Now, don't take all my comments about being in the mirror the wrong way. I'm not a vain person. I was just excited that this situation, which was totally out of my control, was finally going away. With all of the other changes I had been through, it felt good to see one thing going back to normal. However, as my weight began to decrease, I started experiencing another side effect of the steroids: my hair began falling out.

My hair has always been thick. Growing up, my mom kept it relaxed, making it long and easier to manage. Relaxed hair was okay, it just seemed to not do what I wanted half the time. Either I would pay to have it fixed and not like the style, or I would like the style, sleep on it and the hair would be ruined. I also had a few bad hair experiences.

One of those happened the summer I was in high school when I went with my sisters to visit my dad. We didn't get our hair professionally done while we were there because my cousin Rhonda, who was my dad's niece, said she could do our hair herself. Well, of course, it was my luck to go first, and it was a disaster! Rhonda didn't dilute the setting lotion with water before rolling my hair. When I came from under the dryer, my hair was rock hard! Instead of washing my hair and starting over, Rhonda proceeded to rake a comb and brush through my hair. I had to tell her to stop. Needless to say, my hair looked horrible. When I returned home and went to the hairdresser, she told me I had extensive hair damage and ended up cutting my hair all the way to my shoulders to allow it to grow healthy again. It seemed like those types of things were always happening to me. Thus, in college, I decided to go natural.

On the day I wanted to make the "big chop," I went to my friend's house and asked her to do it. She hesitated because she said I would regret it and that she wouldn't be cutting her hair off if her hair was long like mine. As a response, I took the scissors from her hand, grabbed a handful of my hair, and started cutting away. I told her the hair was going so she could either cut it so it looked somewhat even, or I would have to do it. Once she saw I was serious, she began cutting my hair.

Even though she wasn't the only one who thought I was making a big mistake, I didn't care. I loved my fro from the beginning. Once it became longer, I decided I wanted to loc my hair, so I began going to a hairstylist every two weeks to begin the process. No longer did I have to worry about the weather, sleeping, or working out ruining my hair. I didn't even have to worry about styling it because locs were their own style. All I had to do was go to the salon to get my new growth twisted, and I was good to go! So when the steroids began affecting my hair, it was devastating.

Before my hair stylist told me about the damage, I could tell the hair around my edges was thinning. Still, I had been told that as locs grow longer, they could cause hair thinning around the face because of their weight, so I thought it was supposed to happen. I didn't realize it was a problem until my stylist mentioned it. Once she brought it to my attention, it seemed like overnight, my locs began falling out one by one.

My hair thinned so badly that where there were at least ten locs on the side of my face, there ended up being only one. My hairdresser noticed my hair was thinner every time she saw me. To her credit, she did her best to hide what was happening by putting my hair in updos. She also ensured not to pull my locs too tightly. However, the more my hair fell out, the harder it was to cover up.

I woke up one morning, looked in the mirror and decided the only logical thing left to do about my hair was cut it all off. I had so many locs that had fallen out, and my hair looked horrible. I knew the locs wouldn't grow back, so I felt like trying to hang onto hair that was falling out was just my way of avoiding the inevitable. So I took a pair of scissors, went into the bathroom, and cut off my remaining locs. Then I got dressed and walked around the corner to the barbershop to let them take care of the rest.

Me, Nicole and B!

I didn't immediately like the change. I hadn't planned on cutting my hair again and didn't like that the choice was forced upon me. However, as I went to work the next day at the high school I was interning at, the kids told me that I was ready for America's Next Top

Model because of my sexy transformation. Well, I definitely didn't feel sexy, but I appreciated the compliments! I think I was able to take the new hairstyle better because I had my face back. I don't know if things would have been the same if I looked like I did back in December of 2007!

I'm so grateful the kids were nice to me! Battling with my image after cutting my hair was a daily struggle. As I continued to work on loving the new me, the Pam with lupus and short hair, the kids accepted me for who I was because even though my outside had changed, I was still the woman who helped them with their work and listened when they needed someone to talk to.

By this time, I had received all of the bills in the mail from both hospital stays. They amounted to about $15,000! I had no way of paying back all of the money I owed because I made just enough to take care of my rent and other expenses. I began to worry. That's when I remembered the fund NYU has for students with unexpected medical bills. So I went to find out more about it and realized I was eligible to apply. I filled out the forms and submitted them. I was told a committee reviewed all of the applications, and I would receive a letter stating how much money I was awarded.

When I received my letter, I was awarded $9,000 toward my bills! They told me they were sending the money directly to the hospital. I was so grateful to be receiving help because I knew it wasn't something I could pay off on my own. After that, I called and spoke with Dr. Crawford's assistant to begin setting up payment arrangements for the rest of my bill. I explained that I only had a part-time job and didn't have much extra money. He asked me to hold on, and after returning to the phone, he told me that he had spoken with Dr. Crawford. Dr. Crawford had decided to release me from the rest of the money I owed! He told me Dr. Crawford said since he had received most of the money and knew I was a college student, he didn't want me to worry about it. That was absolutely a miracle! Not only had Dr. Crawford been nice to me before each surgery when I was a patient, but this act proved he also cared about me as a person. I cannot tell you how relieved I felt. I asked his assistant to thank him for me.

On May 14, 2008, I graduated from NYU with all As and two Bs! I absolutely believe my faith made that possible. With all that I had gone through, I didn't have to drop or retake any classes, and my GPA from NYU was better than my GPA from studying at U of L when I was healthy and had no medical issues! I was so glad that my hard work had paid off. I was excited to finally be done with school and just focus on working and building a life for myself.

Chapter 5:
Crossroads

Have you ever felt stuck between a rock and a hard place? That you have a decision to make, but not one of the outcomes seems favorable? Well, that's where I found myself less than six months after graduating. I thought I was on my way to a new life, but I was sadly mistaken. To truly understand what I mean, I have to jump back to an event that happened while I was attending the University of Louisville.

I mentioned earlier that I used to sing in the Black Diamond Gospel Choir on U of L's campus. I loved it. We received college credit, which meant during our class time, we had rehearsal for upcoming performances. We mostly sang at churches over the weekend, but we did sing at a women's prison once. I had a group of friends nicknamed the five amigos because we would go to my grandma's house before rehearsal to eat dinner (pack up lots of leftovers) and then go to class together. It felt very much like family.

In 2003, I was told about a worship conference through InterVarsity Christian Fellowship, the Christian group in which I was a student leader. They have the conference every few years. This upcoming conference, happening in the next few months, would be the first time they wanted to include a student choir in the worship team. The leader of our Christian group nominated me as being a good fit for this opportunity. If I agreed to be a part of the conference, which would be December 27-31, I would have to be there a week earlier, which would be during Christmas. I would also have to participate in a few rehearsals in the next couple of months. Even though I was a little bummed that I wouldn't be with my family for Christmas, I was excited about singing and loved conferences, so I said yes.

The first rehearsal was uneventful. I felt good about the songs and started to meet new friends. The second time we gathered, there was a new singer named Jabari. He was tall, had pretty brown skin and a handsome smile. We both noticed one another almost immediately. He would fill the place of another singer who could no longer participate.

Now I was excited about Jabari because I hadn't dated much, and it was hard for me to find attractive men who didn't just say they were a Christian but tried to live that way as well. I've been told I am too picky, but the way I figured it, I was a good catch, so I didn't want to settle for anyone.

I don't remember exactly when we told each other we were interested or exchanged numbers. I just remember getting to know him during the conference (we went everywhere together when we could), and both of us wanted to date each other afterward.

Throughout my time at U of L and NYU, Jabari and I were a couple. He was my first boyfriend. Sometimes I would travel to see him, and sometimes he would travel to see me. Jabari came into town to visit me the weekend I graduated from the University of Louisville. He also flew to New York to help with the apartment after I moved there. When I flew out of town during spring break after getting out of the hospital, I went to see Jabari. So even though the relationship was long distance, he always showed up for the things that mattered to me. And I tried to do the same for him.

Both our families also seemed to be on board. Even though his mom commented about my weight (I was too skinny for her), she seemed to like me. And his sisters and dad were nice as well. My family also seemed to like him. They were pleasant around him and supported the relationship.

We didn't always have to fly to each other's state to be together, though. Since we were both involved in the same Christian group on our respective campuses, we would meet up at the conferences in our region as well. He became my best friend, and I enjoyed our time together. He was never physically present when I was in the hospital, but we always talked on the phone. It seemed he was always available when I called, and he was very supportive.

I had been attending NYU for over a year when Jabari proposed. I knew it would eventually happen, but the way it happened was a surprise. He called me and asked me to call my mom. Then he asked my mom if he could marry me. She said yes, and then he asked me. I said yes. Jabari and I talked about rings over the phone, and then I purchased my engagement ring while I was still in New York.

All of my friends were very happy for me. They wanted to know all the details about the proposal and said my ring was beautiful. Before I left New York, my friends surprised me by throwing me a bridal party. We had a good time.

After graduation, the plan was for Jabari to buy a house in Alabama, where he's from, and then for me to move down after graduation. I didn't mind living in Alabama. I was used to moving every few years and was looking forward to the warmer weather. I was also looking forward to being a wife and a mother. I was so excited about moving that I didn't even stay for my graduation in New York. As soon as I finished classes, I flew back home to get my car and then drove the next day to Alabama to start my new life.

However, things didn't turn out the way I expected. I moved to Alabama in May and returned to New York in August. It seemed Jabari didn't care about any of the things that were important to me.

We weren't hanging out much. He was always telling his mother about the things I did that aggravated him, and he began criticizing me. He would tell me that I embarrassed him with how I dressed. When I would set the table for dinner and put the food in serving bowls, he would comment that I was doing too much and that we could just keep the food in the pots. Even when we hosted dinner for his best friend, and I tried to serve everyone and get all the dishes, he criticized me and allowed his friend to do the same. He even told me after an argument that I would make him hit me.

There was even an instance when a woman claiming to be sleeping with him contacted my younger sister Monica because she wanted to stay in a relationship with him and hoped I would dump him after hearing the news. Well, of course, my sister told me (she spoke to Melissa about it first). I confronted Jabari, and he said it wasn't true. I believed him. His explanation seemed plausible, and I figured he wouldn't be marrying me if he didn't love me.

However, the way he was treating me was wearing on me. I had already talked to him about it, and nothing was changing, so I knew I couldn't stay in the relationship. Part of me wanted to try to make things work (no relationship is perfect), and the other part didn't want to look like a failure because I had already purchased my dress and sent out wedding invitations.

If I were being totally honest, I would say the other reason I wanted to stay is I had finally found someone who loved me. With all the craziness that lupus could bring, I didn't want to give up on the relationship too quickly because I wasn't sure if I could find someone better than him.

However, the more I tried to work on the relationship, the more I noticed I was the only one doing the work. So one morning, I had just had enough. I went to the basement, which was where he was, and gave him back the ring. His response was to ask me if I wanted to throw a party. I just looked at him. I called my mom and sisters, and they were supportive. My mom said she never really liked him in the first place and said I didn't have to stay in Alabama if I didn't want to. Melissa told me I could return to New York to live with her, which is what I did. I believe it was less than a year after we broke up that he was married.

Once I was back in New York, finding a job proved tougher than I thought. The school system in New York went on a hiring freeze, so I couldn't find a job as a counselor.

I did find a job selling Kirby vacuum cleaners, but the work was hard. We were selling door to door and would only receive a paycheck if we made three sales. I only ended up making one sale for myself and two sales for others, so I didn't receive any pay and figured the work I was putting in wasn't worth it.

Once I resigned from that position, I began looking for another opportunity to make money to support myself. One of my friends from church told me about a company that needed temporary call representatives. She said the pay was good, and the company expected to hire some of the temps in a permanent position. I went with her to apply, and once my background check came back, I started working at the call center. The job was really easy. Everyone I spoke to on the phone was nice. I did make money while the agency needed temps, but I wasn't hired on permanently. After about a month, I was out of a job again.

To make matters worse, Melissa and I were notified our apartment was going to be sold. At this time, Melissa decided to move back to DC, which meant I would be in New York by myself and I wasn't sure if I could support myself without a good-paying job. I didn't mind being alone. I just didn't want to struggle financially.

So now we come to the part where I mentioned earlier I felt stuck between a rock and a hard place. I wanted to stay in New York but had no way to support myself. I was still ashamed of my breakup with Jabari, so I didn't want to go home and have to face my family. I didn't want the looks or have to tell people about the details of the breakup. I just wanted to forget that it had ever happened.

Prayer is a big part of my life, so I prayed about where I needed to go. I felt Louisville was the answer I was given. Still, because of the shame I was feeling, I didn't move immediately. I continued to try to find a job, but when I couldn't, I realized the only choice I had was to return home, and I was dreading it.

Thinking back, it was absurd that I felt like a failure just because of a broken relationship, especially when my family had already told me they supported my decision. I think my feelings stemmed from the fact that I had poured so much of my time and energy into the relationship, and I felt like I had wasted many years. I was also suffering from the what-ifs. What if I hadn't met Jabari? How would those five years have been different? What if I hadn't moved right after graduation? Would I have been able to get a job before the hiring freeze?

My diagnosis of lupus was also contributing to these feelings because with the weight gain, hair loss, and knowing I may not be able to have children, I felt unlovable. And here was a person I was leaving who said he loved me. Was I crazy? I felt part of my decision was a mistake and wondered if I could find someone else who would care for me.

However, I kept all this to myself as I tried to hang out with as many friends as possible before returning to Louisville. On one such occasion, I went with a friend as she looked for athletic shoes. I wasn't into tennis shoes at the time, but I figured I'd look silly just standing in one spot, so I browsed through the rows of shoes. As I looked at the shoes, just knowing I wouldn't find anything that would interest me, I came across some grey Converse sneakers. They were awesome! They were a dark grey, which happens to be one of my favorite colors, made of wool, with a neat checkered pattern. I tried them on, and I loved the way they looked. Things got even better because they were also on sale! My friend saw me trying them on and came over for a better look. She encouraged me to buy them.

I bring this up because I wasn't in the right frame of mind when I walked into the shoe store. I was struggling with moving back to Louisville, and I didn't even want to look around the store because I was sure I wouldn't see anything I liked.

However, this is where choice comes in. I didn't have a choice about the lupus. I didn't have a choice about Jabari forgetting me so quickly. I didn't have a choice about staying in my current apartment. But, what I did have a choice on was my mindset. And so do you.

We will always have the choice to choose how we respond to the circumstances in our life. I think I felt so devastated about how my life was turning out that I didn't remember that I still had a choice. Looking at those shoes and liking them was the turning point for me.

Before purchasing them, I was not one to wear sneakers. It was not my thing. The only athletic shoes I had were my workout shoes. So finding a pair of sneakers in that store made me realize the new Pamala likes the sneakers, and that is a good thing. And if I can open myself up to liking something I had never liked before and enjoy the moment, what else can I accomplish? I went into the store feeling stuck. However, after seeing the shoes, I saw myself in a new way and recognized I could begin again. I could go back home and reconnect with friends I missed seeing while in New York. I could be happy again and create new goals and dreams for my life.

And most importantly, I could work on my self-esteem and start to love the person staring at me in the mirror even though I didn't recognize her. I knew that if I purchased the shoes, that would be a sign of me letting go of who I used to be and learning to love who I was becoming. And in that moment, that was all that mattered. So I purchased the shoes and decided to walk into my new life with my head held high!

Feeling good about my upcoming transition, I began to apply for jobs so that once I arrived in Louisville, I could begin to work right away. I applied for a job at St. Joseph Children's Home (St. Joe's) and a few days later received a call. I explained to the supervisor, Bobbi, I was still in New York but would be in Louisville on the fourth of November. She set up an interview for me, and I told her I looked forward to seeing her soon.

I also began looking online for a ticket. Because I was relocating on Election Day, I found a one-way ticket to Louisville for under $100! After I bought that plane ticket, it seemed like everything was finally falling into place. There was no turning back now. No deciding to stay in New York. No returning to the old relationship. No going back to the old Pam. My new destiny was in front of me, and it was up to me how I would handle it. I could continue to be sad about what I had lost or be grateful for the things I still had. I chose the latter.

I was truly starting to feel like I was on my way. New beginnings were waiting for me, and I was excited about my upcoming transition back home. Now that I felt like my extreme makeover was beginning from the inside out, I was ready to go!

Part II
Living with Lupus

೮೮೮೮೮೮

L.U.P.U.S—Lives Unlocking Powerful Unexpected Strength; it may cause optimism, more afternoon naps, experimentation with new hairstyles, an excuse to flaunt your derby hat all year round, and more shopping sprees.

೮೮೮೮೮೮

This part of my memoir is about motivation. Along my journey, I found I still had something to give despite my diagnosis. Now that you know the life-changing event I went through, I want to encourage you to keep pushing forward as I show you how I moved from being overwhelmed with lupus to being an overcomer.

Chapter 6:
Losing My Voice to Find It

I enjoyed a smooth airplane ride into Louisville. My grandmother welcomed me back into her apartment with open arms. It felt really good to be back! The night I arrived, one of my friends, Mariam, invited me to an election party. We had so much fun! Not only did Obama win, but we met some first-time voters and enjoyed some delicious food!

The day I arrived in Louisville with my grey sneakers on!

I fell back into my old routine of helping my grandmother and eating her delicious food! I secured a job at St. Joe's and bought a car, so things were becoming more comfortable. A few months after arriving in Louisville, I remembered the Lupus Foundation of America.

I first heard about the Lupus Foundation of America, LFA, through their magazine, Lupus Now. Melissa gave me my first subscription to the magazine after I was diagnosed with lupus. It was the only lupus magazine at the time (that I knew of) that talked about the newest research studies and breakthroughs concerning lupus. It also had a men's page that answered questions men had about their struggles with lupus. In the back of the magazine were all of the LFA chapters in the United States. That's where I found information for the Mid-South Chapter, which is over the state of Kentucky.

I began calling Sherry Hammond, the president and CEO at the time. There weren't any lupus programs, support groups, or activities being held in Louisville. Since I was feeling good, I figured I could start volunteering to start a program or event. When Sherry and I spoke, she informed me two other ladies were also interested in starting programs and events in Louisville, and she invited me to meet them in April. I didn't know anyone who was living with lupus yet, so I was excited to meet some new people who could relate to me.

I met Sherry Hammond in person, as well as her Walk Coordinator, Mary Self, and the other two volunteers over lunch. As the five of us sat and discussed ideas, Sherry stated she would like to start a walk in Louisville. We all agreed that would be a great idea. She then looked at me and told me she wanted me to be over the walk. I excitedly said I would, and Sherry created an email for me and ordered me business cards. In all my excitement, I didn't think about how much work it would take to be over a walk in Louisville. I had no experience in fundraising or soliciting volunteers, so the first few months were hard. It seemed like I was putting in a lot of time without having much to show for it. And I was nervous that I might have set myself up for failure because I wasn't securing any donations or volunteers. Once I spoke to Mary about my concerns, she began working with me. It didn't take long before we had organized our first walk committee.

Everyone on the committee was excited about the walk, and we all began to work together. We all had some connection to lupus: some had lupus, while others had family members with lupus. I think this made us stronger. We had a vested interest in finding a cure. Even though we were put over different aspects of the event—food and beverage, volunteers, team captains, etc., we still worked as a group.

For our first event, we were expecting around 250 people. We chose a small park, one that would be easily accessible for those in wheelchairs, and our walk was held in September on a Saturday morning. To help promote the walk, I was invited to speak on a local TV station as well as the radio.

Besides going on speaking engagements, we began reaching out to different stores in the community for donations. We were able to receive food, water, and soda donations. We also contacted family and friends for monetary donations to help us reach our walk goal. Some of the same businesses that donated the first year we had our walk continued to donate throughout the years.

About a month before our first walk, we had our launch party, which was designed to help motivate our sponsors and team captains to continue to fundraise and grow their teams. We had great food, door prizes, and lots of information. I was given the opportunity to share my story with all those present. That was the first time I publicly spoke about being diagnosed with lupus. Afterward, I was complimented on my speech as well as my delivery. And that's when I realized that maybe some good could come from my diagnosis. That I could use my story to motivate others. I might not have had the voice I was used to, but I still had one that needed to be used. So, I started to think of ways I could motivate others during the walk.

I love writing, so the first thing that came to mind was creating a T-shirt with a catchy motivational phrase or logo. At the time, the symbol for the LFA was a purple butterfly, so I knew I would have that on my T-shirt. And as I continued to look at the word lupus, my acronym was born—L.U.P.U.S., which stands for "lives unlocking powerful unexpected strength." The T-shirt came out wonderful! On the front was my butterfly and then the definition of lupus, which is negative. On the back, I had my acronym for lupus and a definition that gave a positive for every negative in the definition on the front. There was also a scripture on the back. I loved the shirt because it was a visual reminder that everything in life was about mindset. We could choose either the negative or positive. And I was determined to choose the latter!

My mindset about my diagnosis was changing. I didn't have to let my diagnosis determine who I would be and what I would achieve. Instead, it unlocked in me the strength I never knew I possessed that propelled me toward obtaining new goals. I began to discover that as long as I kept a positive mindset, even with lupus, nothing would be impossible for me.

Me at the first launch party, sharing my story!

The first walk was a success! We had double the number of people than we expected because of the publicity, and many people complimented us and said they couldn't wait for next year's walk. That first year my team was tiny, consisting of my sister Monica, my good friend Mariam, and me. Monica and Mariam helped where needed, and I was glad they were there to support me.

We had face painting and an area just for the kids. We had free food and hot coffee. We had giveaways. It was definitely a family-friendly event. Pets were also welcome! The event is called a walk because sometimes, when someone has lupus, their energy is low, so we wanted to be sure everyone who wanted to could participate. We even had cheerleaders stationed around the trail, cheering everyone on and handing out water.

We all wore the T-shirt I created, and I began selling it online as well.

Monica, Me, and Mariam at the first Lupus Walk.

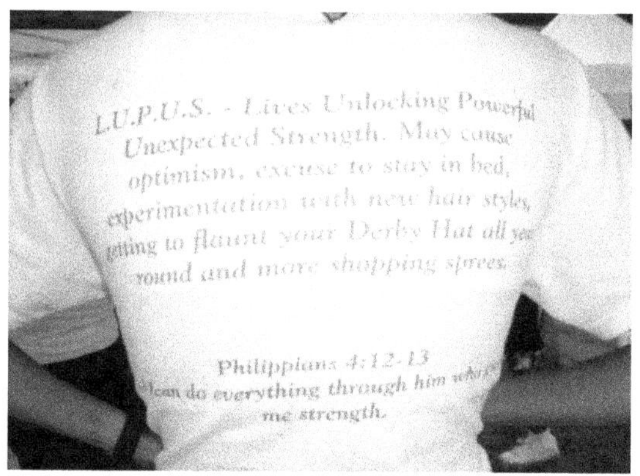

The back of the T-shirt I created.

Two months after the walk, we began planning for the 2010 walk. I was asked to be the walk chair again, and I gladly accepted. Also, most of the walk committee stayed on for the next year, so planning the new walk wasn't that bad.

As the years progressed, I continued to be the walk chair and use my voice to encourage others. I also went on the radio, TV, and I was a representative for the LFA at many health fairs. The best part about using my voice to motivate others was the speaking engagements.

My first speaking engagement was at a local church for their Women's Day service. The women had decided to raise money in support of the LFA and asked a representative to come and share about lupus. Sherry said she would like me to go, so I began working on my speech. I was nervous once I arrived at the church. As I looked around, I didn't see any familiar faces. There was a table in the hallway for me to use for the LFA materials, so I stood there in case anyone had questions. Someone came when it was almost time for me to speak. I'm a bit of a perfectionist, so I practiced my speech so much that I had it memorized! Many people came up to me afterward and told me how touched they were by my story and told me of women they knew who had lupus. My experiences that day reaffirmed how powerful it is when you share your story with others. Most of us don't look like what we have gone through. Once someone hears your story and sees you in your present, it gives them hope that they can make it out of their struggles as well.

So, I continued to take advantage of those opportunities because I could see how my story impacted others. Any chance I got, I used it to motivate those living with lupus. My mom, who lived in a different state, would sometimes even call me asking if she could give my number to someone she met with lupus! So, sharing my story was becoming a lifestyle. All this sharing allowed me to come out of my shell and not be so shy.

Before my diagnosis, I was shy and had trouble with public speaking. My diagnosis changed that aspect of my life. I now had a story others wanted to hear and a message I wanted to share with anyone who would listen: unexpected circumstances don't have to be the end of your story. They can be the beginning. And who would have thought this new voice I have would be used for public speaking? Certainly not me!

When I was in the hospital for the second time, there was a point where I became very hoarse, and my voice went away for about a day. When it returned, it was a raspy mess, and I just figured once I felt better, my voice would return to normal. Well, it never did.

This is one of the reasons I was having such a hard time accepting the new Pam: I didn't sound like myself. There are things about ourselves that we are known for or that make up our unique identities. Some of us are known for our fashion. Some of us are known for our personalities. Some of us are known for our connections and circle of friends. One of the things that made up a big part of my identity was my voice.

Singing was a big part of my life. I used to teach the children's choir new songs and sing with them. I used to sing in church as part of the young adult ministry and when I went away for mission trips. I sang in the Black Diamond Gospel Choir. After hearing me, some people were shocked that I sounded so good. One person even mentioned I sang like an angel. So singing wasn't just something that I did. It was a big part of who I was.

More so than that, you hear your voice every day. Whether I was talking to myself or someone else, that small task was a constant reminder of my diagnosis of lupus and that I wasn't the same. I could no longer sing and put smiles on the faces of others. And even though I was working on being okay with the new Pam, the process took time. Hearing my voice sometimes made me sad because it was a constant reminder that one of the things I loved to do was taken away from me.

However, once I started working with the LFA, my voice was given a new purpose. I could share my story. I could educate and encourage those with lupus and their caregivers. I could still bring smiles to people's faces, just in a different way. Having to endure a life-changing event doesn't automatically mean your quality of life will be worse in the future. Whether your life-changing event was a breakup, illness, loss of income or anything else, each day we wake up is another chance to fulfill our dreams. Another chance to reexamine our lives. Another chance to help someone in need. Another chance to create our own happiness!

And this is possible when you shift your mindset. With a great mindset and will to bring new meaning to your life, you will start to see that even though things have changed, your life still has a purpose. And you'll discover, like I did, an unexpected power to engage and conquer new tasks you never thought of completing. My new voice, this purposeful voice, although weak and frail at times, was full of power and I wanted to make sure it stayed that way!

BEGIN NOW

What negative change have you endured that you could turn into a positive attribute?

CHAPTER 7:
PAMALA

I was becoming used to my voice and no longer caring about how it sounded since it was helping those around me. I was also becoming used to my body. In February 2010, all the extra weight that the steroids added to my frame was gone, and I was the same size I was before my second surgery. I cannot tell you how happy I was to be little again. My rheumatologist told me that I was a bit thin (which made sense because I had lost weight while I was in the hospital), but he said as long as I was eating and not trying to lose weight, it was fine.

However, I began to be obsessed with my weight. I would wake up in the mornings and look at my body in the mirror to ensure I hadn't gained any weight. Gone were the days I went back for seconds or filled my plate. This progressed to me eating fewer meals a day until I only ate one full meal a day. When I did eat, I ate mostly fruit or yogurt because I didn't want to take in too many calories. I knew what I was doing to myself was wrong, but it was something I had control over. When I had to take the medicine that made me gain weight, I couldn't control how much weight I gained or how fast it came off. I felt helpless.

However, now that I did have control, and even though I wasn't using my control in a healthy way, it felt good to be in charge of my body again. Still, my family and friends started commenting about how much and what I was eating. One of my cousins would comment that I was only eating fruit or smoothies. So I started to tell my family that I had already eaten at family gatherings. That way, the comments would stop.

However, then the comments started from others as well. One of my church members told me I was the skinniest person he'd ever seen. I went home and looked at myself in the mirror, and I could see almost all of my ribs. I was just trying not to gain weight. I didn't realize in the process, I had become too skinny. It was then that I decided something needed to change. So I began to force myself to eat three meals a day. I didn't want to make the lupus any worse. I also began to research healthy diets and learn how to cook healthy meals so that I could maintain the body that I wanted in a way that wasn't jeopardizing my health.

So not only did I struggle with my physical image, but I also struggled mentally. I didn't fully love myself. I didn't love the new

Pam. I knew I wouldn't die any sooner because of lupus, but I felt no one would want to be in a relationship with me or love me because there was something wrong with me. There's no cure for lupus, and there's no way to plan for flare-ups (what happens when lupus attacks your body). You can become sick at any moment, and that is scary to some people. More so, I had tests done, and I was told I might be unable to have children.

You have to understand that before I was diagnosed with lupus, I rarely became sick. I was always active in sports, and I could pretty much do anything I wanted. There was a time in undergrad when I worked out twice a day and ran two miles every day on the treadmill. It was hard trying to get used to not being as active and now having limitations with working out.

Another part of my mental struggle was wishing I was the old Pamala: to be a track star, to sing first soprano in the choir, and not to become sick every winter. However, that wish never came true. I knew I had to be the new Pam to motivate others, but I was having a hard time forgetting how things used to be and trying to embrace my new challenges. There were so many new things when I moved back to Louisville that I didn't really have time to focus on all of the changes I had been through. However, as things started to slow down and I had more time, all the changes were starting to weigh on me, and I felt like I might be unable to realize all my dreams.

I wish I could say I woke up one morning, and suddenly, I loved myself, but it wasn't that easy. Every morning I had to make a conscious effort to tell myself that I was wonderful the way I was. I didn't love the new me, but I committed to beginning the journey of rediscovering myself, hoping to one day unconditionally love the face I now saw in the mirror.

Over time, instead of going through the motions of loving myself, I began to do just that: love Pamala, the one with the raspy voice, weakened joints, and low immune system. I no longer yearned to be who I was before because who I was becoming was more appealing to me. I was beginning to like the compliments I received about my voice. I enjoyed acting in plays. I looked forward to my LFA speaking engagements. I was learning to tell people no so that I could get the rest I needed. And that's one of the things I liked the best!

I've always been a busy person. Whether active in sports or volunteering, I was rarely at home. Once I began volunteering with an organization and they saw how well I did, they would ask me to volunteer for more things. I would always say yes because I usually had the time, and it was fun. However, after my diagnosis, I realized I needed to be sure I was giving myself enough resting time. Because of this, I had to learn to tell people no. And, no, I didn't just tell people I had lupus to get out of things I was supposed to do. I just began telling the different organizations that I wouldn't be able to commit further than what I had already agreed upon.

And a funny thing happened after I started telling people no. They accepted it! In my mind, I thought I would receive a lot of backlash for not doing more, but people were very understanding. And another thing I realized is I don't always have to explain myself to others.

Now, if you haven't already guessed, I love to talk! And I'm usually trying to tell all the details when I'm letting someone know about something that happened to me. Well, anytime I changed my mind or didn't want to do something, I would try to explain myself so the person I was no longer going to help would know I had a legitimate excuse. However, I realized I didn't owe anyone an explanation. I could tell someone no thank you and be done with the conversation there.

I'm telling you all this because as I learned to become adjusted to my new life, I also found a new level of confidence in myself. That confidence allowed me to decide to rest when I needed and tell people no when I didn't want to over-commit myself. And this wasn't something I had the confidence to do before my diagnosis.

This new confidence was another thing I learned to love about the new me. And each day I walked along on this new journey, I began to see more reasons to continue doing the work to love myself. I realized even though I couldn't workout three times a day, I could workout once a day. I realized even though I became sick easier, I was giving myself more time to rest. I realized even though this new Pamala was different, different doesn't always mean worse.

I've honestly always been different, and it started at my birth. My name is Pamala. All As, no E. I cannot tell you how many times I've spelled my name aloud for people, and they still spelled it wrong. Growing up, I corrected my teachers so much about my name that they began calling me Pam because they didn't want to remember how to spell Pamala. This is part of why I prefer to be called Pamala and not Pam. However, the point I'm trying to make is the spelling of my name is different. Not bad, just different. And if I could develop confidence about my name, get in the habit of spelling my name for people, and learn to correct them when they spelled it wrong, I could learn to live with lupus.

It's all about your mindset. Being diagnosed with lupus was different for me, but it didn't have to be bad. I didn't have to think that my life was over or that I wouldn't be able to accomplish my dreams. I just needed to create a new path for myself. I needed to write a new story for my life.

And in this new story, I could not only accomplish dreams I had before my diagnosis, but I could create new dreams for myself as well. Yes, I would have challenges because of the lupus and yes, life had definitely changed for me, but I was still the same person. My smile was still the same. I still laughed the same way, and my personality was still the same. I was still me, Pamala, with three As, and I was still determined to set and conquer my goals.

Life after lupus didn't have to be scary and uneventful. Life after lupus could be filled with strength. Not just strength to help me get through my hard times but strength to give to others to help push them along on their journey. My diagnosis of lupus had always been bigger than me!

To this day, as every new challenge comes, I have to face my limitations and ask myself if I'll become negative because of something I seemingly cannot do or if I will find a way to be an achiever despite lupus. Most of the time, I choose the latter. I still have to go to see my team of doctors, take my medications, and I still have days when I don't feel well. I'm just choosing to smile through these times instead of grumble.

Around February 2011, I received great news from my rheumatologist during one of my appointments. I sincerely believe I have one of the best rheumatologists in the country, and his name is Dr. Gary Crump. I see him every six months and always look forward to it. We talk about our dogs. He lets me know about cool spots to hang out in Louisville and always has a smile on his face. I've even brought him baked goods! He is pretty popular, so I usually have to wait before seeing him. However, even if he is running behind, I don't mind because when he comes into the room, he doesn't rush me, and we end up having good conversations.

So, during this appointment, once Dr. Crump entered the room, he asked me how I was doing, and he checked my hands and ankles for swelling. I told him I felt great. He usually tells me I am his healthiest patient because, usually, when I see him, I feel great, and my labs are good. He picked up my chart and began to read. After a few minutes, he told me I was in remission! He said there was no lupus activity in my body. Talk about receiving the best news of your life! I couldn't believe I was in remission after everything I had gone through.

Once I left his office, I shared the news with my friends and family and church. Everyone was so happy for me! It felt good to have so many people wishing me well. To this day, I am still in remission!

Whatever you are going through, don't give up! Things may be different, but that doesn't mean they are bad. We just have to find new ways of dealing with the challenges in our lives. Just like life can throw negative circumstances our way, life can bring positive experiences as well. Our mindset is what gets us through them all. Choose to smile. Choose to have a positive outlook. Choose to keep moving forward to conquer your dreams. And who knows, you may be surprised about how good life can become!

Begin Now

What areas of your life do you need to develop self-confidence in?

CHAPTER 8:
JUST BREATHE

Now that I was in remission, I started looking for a gym because I wanted to start working out again. I started running track in kindergarten and continued participating in sports throughout middle and high school. Some of those sports included track, volleyball, and softball. In undergrad, I tried out for the rowing team and made it, but I quit soon after because we practiced several times a day, and I wouldn't have had time for anything else. And while I lived in New York, I was working on becoming a personal trainer. So, throughout my life, I've always been active.

There were several gyms to choose from, but I was looking for something specific. One of the interesting things about lupus is you don't look sick. So, no one assumes anything is wrong with me. Because of this, I didn't want to be at a gym where I felt I would always have to explain myself in class if I wasn't pushing myself hard. I wanted a gym for all kinds of people so that even on my bad days, I would still feel accepted and included. In my search for gyms, I went on many tours. During one of them, when I asked if they had any fitness classes like water aerobics (which is good for someone who has joint pain), the tour guide laughed and said they didn't because classes like that were for old people. I told him I had lupus and that classes like that were perfect for me. He didn't say anything else. Needless to say, that was the first and last time I stepped foot in that particular chain of gyms. The gym that ended up being the best fit for me was the YMCA.

When I first started working out, I focused a lot on yoga because my doctors explained that yoga would be good for my joints. I was also told I was at a higher risk for osteoporosis, and yoga would help with that too. As I got the hang of being a yogi and gained some strength, I tried other types of exercises like weight lifting, Pilates, and spinning classes.

Pilates ended up becoming one of my favorite classes. When my schedule allowed, I went twice a week on Mondays and Thursdays. I made new friends and started to see myself become more toned because of the workouts. I eventually shared with the instructor my diagnosis, and she would always ask me if I felt okay if I was using modifications. She's very sweet!

Once I had been a member of the Y for a few years, I decided to shake things up and try some new classes. Anyone who works out knows you can't continue to do the same thing repeatedly because you'll plateau and no longer see results. So I knew I needed to try some new things. I had heard a lot about a dance class on Wednesday nights, so I knew I wanted to check it out. Then I chose a more challenging class, Cardo F.I.T., taught by the same instructor, Sonny. Sonny is the absolute best fitness instructor I've ever met. His classes are challenging, fun, and some of the most popular. I've created for myself a small family at the Y, and Sonny has been a big part of why that happened.

Even more than Sonny being an awesome person, I also felt comfortable telling him I had lupus. When he knew I was injured or was low energy, he made sure I was taking care of myself. One example of this was I ended up injuring my knees one day at the gym. I ran for a couple of miles on the treadmill and ended up overworking my knees. I had to get X-rays and everything. However, since I had injured myself, I absolutely had to take it slow and stay away from any sort of exercise that was high-impact. Sonny shows modifications all the time for his class, so I could continue going on Wednesday nights.

So, on the day that I told him I needed to take it slow, as some of my favorite high-impact songs started to play since my knees weren't hurting then, I was jumping around just like normal. And then suddenly, I heard Sonny calling me out on his microphone in front of the class because I wasn't taking it slow. I was a bit embarrassed but appreciative that he reminded me of what I needed to do.

After the class ended, I went up to talk to him like I normally did, and he explained he had knee injuries and wanted me to take care of myself so I could be around for a long time. Sonny is so sweet! He's one of three people who are allowed to call me Pammy.

In 2015, I landed my first job in higher education as an academic advisor. My new job focused heavily on being healthy. We even had a health and wellness committee! One of the coolest things my employer would do is pay ten dollars toward my Y membership, which the Y matched. So that meant my monthly membership fees were cut in half! The other thing my employer would do is pay part of the registration fees for local fitness events to help encourage us to be healthy. There was a limit on how many events we could do each year, but I still thought it neat that it was something they offered. I didn't take them up on it at first because I was still getting used to my new classes at the gym. It wasn't until March 2016 that I participated in my first 5K event, the Leprechaun Run.

What appealed to me about this event was I could either run or walk. You could also choose the length you wanted to complete-either the 5k or 10k. Many of my co-workers were planning on going since our boss would pay the whole registration fee. However, the absolute best part was Maggie, my four-legged child, was allowed to come and would receive a bib as well. I ended up making her a green t-shirt for the occasion so we could be twins!

To prepare for this event, I began my training. I thought it would be cool to run some of it, but at the very least, I wanted to walk the whole 5K distance without any pain in my knees. To do this, I needed to work on my endurance so that my knees would be okay with the long distance.

Now, one thing you have to understand is I was told, after being diagnosed with lupus, that I wouldn't be able to run again. It was a shock at first because I'd been running since kindergarten. My doctor explained that with the stress that running puts on the body and the problems I was having with my joints, my body wouldn't be able to withstand it. I listened to Dr. Crump but secretly told myself that I would prove him wrong, that I would be able to run again.

So the first thing I started doing was walking on the track in the gym. Even though I had been working out for a few years, I needed to start my training slowly. So a few days during the week, I would walk a couple of laps. Since the track was inside, it was very small, so you had to walk around it more than ten times to complete one mile. I would usually just walk around it two to three times at the beginning.

After I felt my body was used to walking more, I started to walk and jog around the track. I would walk half of a lap and then jog the other half. My body seemed to be adjusting well.

I was about a month into training when I decided I would use the Couch to 5K app (C25K) to help prepare me the rest of the way. This app is designed to help people who aren't active become active enough to complete a 5K successfully. So I figured it would be a helpful tool for me.

The app starts you off slowly, so when I started on day one, it was easy for me to accomplish the task. It wasn't until I had progressed far enough in the app to where I was jogging most of the time instead of walking that my knees started to hurt.

When it first happened, I just thought to myself no big deal. I'll give my knees some time off and get right back to it. However, after a few days of rest, my knees weren't any better. A week went by, and then two. It was almost a month before the pain went away. After this happened the first time, I just brushed it off and thought no worries, it would just take longer than expected for me to get to the point of running. Still, as I continued this cycle of starting the app and having to stop because of my knees, I realized it was too soon for me to think about running. There was no need for me to cry because it seemed like the doctor was right that I'd never be able to run again. I just needed to breathe.

Deep breathing has so many benefits for the body. During workouts, it can be important to take deep breaths to slow your heart rate. Also, focusing on your breath in yoga is vital to that practice. Deep breathing also helps with your blood pressure, immune system energy, and stress levels.

Being stress-free is something I've been told I need to be conscious of because of the lupus. When someone with lupus is stressed, the body can start to have flare-ups, which is when the lupus becomes active in the body, and the person becomes sick. The type of lupus I have can affect any part of the body. With a flare-up, you never know what sort of attack you will have. So staying away from anything that can cause a flare-up is what I try to do daily. Deep breathing helps me.

When I know that I have a busy day ahead of me, I will sometimes take deep breaths. I'll pause in the mornings, think about what I have to accomplish and try to breathe away any anxiety I have about the day. If I am about to start a difficult task or walk into a situation that has the potential to be stressful, I will pause long enough to take a few deep breaths. Acknowledging the difficulty ahead of time and pausing to breathe and take an inventory of my body (if it's already starting to feel tense) definitely helps.

Try deep breathing the next time you feel upset or stressed. You can breathe in through your nose and out through your mouth or vice versa. The main thing is to focus on your breathing to calm yourself down. One of the best benefits of using this coping skill is it doesn't cost any money. You already know how to do it, and you can do it anywhere!

So, I breathed. With each breath, I reminded myself that walking led to jogging and jogging led to running. I reminded myself that I still have lots of time to work on running. I reminded myself that I was healthy and in remission. Afterward, there was no reason for me to be upset. I changed my mindset to focus on the positive, and for the rest of my training, I walked so that I would be able to accomplish my goal of finishing the race.

On the day of the race, the participants were allowed to leave work early to change. We also decided to meet up once we were there for pictures. Once the race began, our group split up. Some decided to run while the rest of us walked.

We had a great time! The weather was nice, and it felt good to be out of the office early. I was able to walk the entire distance without overworking my knees! I had officially completed my first 5K without stopping and was extremely proud of myself! I was also proud of Maggie because she behaved around the other dogs.

And the most important thing is I accomplished my goal of running! No, I didn't run during the event, but I did run during my training. There were several days that I ran short distances. It took some work, and I couldn't go far, but I ran. And that means I won. I won my mental battle of not letting myself get down from hearing the news from my doctor. I won my physical struggle of continuing forward when my knees were overworked. I won because I didn't give up. And you can win too.

Any dream you have is worth achieving. It doesn't matter if achieving it takes you longer than expected. It doesn't even matter if you have to modify the dream. All that matters is you try. We have to keep going when life changes happen to us. The most amazing thing about people is how adaptable we are. And what allows us to excel at adapting to new situations is our mindset.

You can tell yourself that life is no longer worth it, or you can tell yourself this isn't something I expected, but I will keep moving forward anyway. Keep going when those around you tell you it's not possible. Keep going when people don't understand. Keep going when you feel discouraged. As long as you have the mindset to keep moving forward toward your dreams, nothing will be impossible for you!

Moreover, you may just realize that some of the dreams you had before your life event are still attainable. One of those dreams for me was to have a pet. I would be doing myself a huge injustice if I didn't dedicate a chapter to one of the best things that have happened to me: being a dog mom to Maggie.

BEGIN NOW

What dream(s) do you have that you still feel is/are attainable, and what steps can you take to achieve your dream(s)?

CHAPTER 9:
MAGGIE

I've always wanted a dog. When I was little, we had two Yorkies named Chip and Duncan. I don't remember how long we had them, but I liked them. Then, in middle school, we had good friends who owned a golden retriever, and when we were at their house, we always played with the dog. So I knew I eventually wanted my own dog when I was older. I just wanted to wait until I was done with school and could afford one.

Around 2013 I started praying about a dog. I also did my research! I have allergies, so I wanted a hypoallergenic dog. I've always had a fascination with Pomeranians. However, I realized I didn't want a dog that would shed. So, as I was researching different breeds, I decided I wanted a Bichon Frise because they didn't shed. They were cute and small and would be a good breed for an apartment.

I started looking online and in the shelters to see if I could spot the dog I was looking for. Even though I had settled on a specific breed, I was still open to others. I also began setting money aside in anticipation of finding my dog.

I volunteer a lot at church, and most of that time is spent with the Children's Church ministry. I work on the bulletins and help plan and coordinate events. As the kids come in and are dropped off, I've gotten to know their families. With one particular child, her mom sometimes brought their dog, Sharpay, with them.

Sharpay was so cute! I didn't know what type of breed she was, but she was really fluffy and had reddish-brown fur. She always seemed happy to see me, and I would pick her up and just love on her for as long as I could. Sometimes her owner would tell me she was bad because she was using the bathroom in the house or tearing up their pillows. She would always say she would give her away. When this happened, I would tell her, if she was going to get rid of Sharpay, to call me because I would take her. I would always say it jokingly, but, of course, there's truth in humor!

Well, I hadn't seen Sharpay for about a year, and I had forgotten about her. Children's Church is only for children in grades first through fifth. So, after fifth grade, the family moved on to middle school.

It was around the end of August 2015. I was working at Children's Church, like I was in the habit of doing, and Ms. Yalanda, the director, came to me and slapped a piece of paper down on the table in front of me with a number on it. She told me I needed to call the number. I was initially nervous because there was no name, so I had no idea why I had to call or who it was. She said it was the dog lady. She was referring to Sharpay's owner! I believe everything happens for a reason. It was definitely not a coincidence that Sharpay's owner was offering her to me as I was looking for a dog.

When I arrived home, the first thing I did was call the number. Sharpay's owner explained they were moving and couldn't take the dog. She said she knew I would care for her, so she wanted to ask me first if I wanted her. She told me she would give her to me for free and also give me her supplies. We spoke on the phone on a Thursday, and she had to be rid of the dog by Sunday, so I didn't have much time to get ready.

I drove out on Sunday to get Sharpay. When I entered the apartment, I saw a dog, but it didn't look anything like I remembered Sharpay looking, so I kept looking around to see where she was. However, Sharpay's owner saw me looking around and told me the dog I saw was Sharpay. I didn't recognize her because her hair was blonde and overgrown.

The family let me know Sharpay would whine at the door if she wanted to go outside and that she liked eggs. They mixed eggs in with her dog food. They told me she didn't know any commands but that she was no longer using the bathroom in the house. They also told me they kept her caged during the day while they weren't there and then at night because of the chewing. I was told Sharpay usually cried when she was put in her cage.

They gave me her bed, food and snacks but the rest of her belongings were packed up since they were moving, so I didn't receive anything else. I made sure to ask about her temperament around kids and dogs, and I also asked about her shot record. I was given records that seemed to show Sharpay wasn't up to date on her shots, so I knew I needed to get her checked out right away. She told me if I took Sharpay to the vet, she would pay half of her medical bills. She also explained that in three months, they would be able to take the dog back if I didn't want her. So it would be a trial. That made me feel good because I was slightly nervous about taking the dog. Things were happening quicker than I would have liked!

Before we left, I was told it would be the first time Sharpay wouldn't be around one of her family members. Still, we walked to the car, and Sharpay jumped in the front seat. Her owner waved to her, and Sharpay looked out the window. And we were off!

That first day I discovered she liked riding in the car! Instead of taking her home, we went directly to the vet. She needed a bath and trim, and I wanted to be sure she didn't have fleas or anything. I took her to the Banfield Pet Hospital inside Pet Smart. Before I picked her up, I spoke to my mom and sister Monica on the phone because they have dogs. Both told me they took their dogs to Banfield Pet Hospital, so I figured if they loved it, I would probably like it as well.

Once inside, I explained what was happening and asked for an appointment. Within a few minutes, we were seen. In the doctor's office, the veterinarian checked Sharpay over and gave her shots. She told me I would have to wait 72 hours to ensure she wouldn't have an allergic reaction before she could go to the groomer. She also noticed her ears were black on the inside and told me she had a serious ear infection. The vet cleaned out her ears and gave me medicine for them. She also checked Sharpay for fleas. Once our appointment was over, I purchased some food, dog bowls and other supplies for Sharpay.

Sharpay played fetch, and the first time she needed to go outside, she stood by the door and whined. She looked really happy once she was inside. However, even though she looked happy, I noticed she wasn't eating her food, and she didn't seem like she was sleeping either. I thought it was because she missed her old owners, but I realized it was because she needed to be groomed! As soon as we came from the groomer, Sharpay went to sleep! She looked like a totally different dog!

I was nervous about Sharpay chewing my shoes and pillows, so I kept her caged at night and during the day the first two days. However, I would come home from work, and my neighbors would tell me she cried all day. I didn't want her to be sad, so I decided to leave her out the third night to see what she would do. I woke up in the morning, and a torn tissue was on the floor. Sharpay had gotten it off of the table. That wasn't a big deal because I knew she was a curious dog, so I decided to keep her out that day while I was a work. I didn't want her to be caged all the time because I always saw myself with a pet that had free roam of my apartment. So I said a little prayer, went to work, and when I returned home, I found her sleeping on the couch. She's been out of her cage at night and during the day ever since! Most nights, she prefers to sleep in bed with me.

After I had Sharpay for about a month, I started thinking of a new name for her. I had learned by then that she really loved being outside, so I researched dog names that were outdoorsy and came across Maggie. Sharpay was sitting beside me one day, and I turned to her and said, "Mags!" She immediately turned around and looked at me. I knew that would be her name!

In October, one of my coworkers told me about a church named First Unitarian that had a service for animal blessings. I immediately told myself I would go and take Maggie because I felt it would be good for her to have a blessing from the pastor. We went for Maggie's blessing on October 4th, and I saw my coworker there with her family and her dog, who happens to be named Maggie as well. My Maggie sometimes doesn't do well with other dogs, so when we went, she was barking and unable to sit still because of all the pets. She did settle down long enough for the pastor to bless her with good health and a long life, but we didn't stay after the service for the dinner because she was being too wild! However, once we got home, I commemorated the moment by putting a bow in her hair and taking a picture!

The day Maggie got her animal blessing!

Maggie and I didn't get along initially. Her previous owners hadn't taught her any commands, so Maggie was not for it when I was trying to teach her to sit, stay, and come. I think part of the issue was she didn't trust me yet. There were times when Maggie completely ignored me and other times when I would have sworn she was talking back to me. The struggle was definitely real! In trying to train Maggie, I realized the best way to have her do what I say is to feed her. She loves food! Now most dogs will have an upset stomach if they eat new foods often but not Maggie. So, after finding this out, not only did training go a lot smoother, but I started giving her human food to see what she liked. Maggie loves sweet potatoes, boiled eggs, tuna, green beans, all meats, oatmeal, yogurt, and ice cream. To this day, Maggie gets organic sweet potatoes in the morning before I go to work!

Maggie isn't trained to use the bathroom inside on a pad, so we take many daily walks. When it started getting cold outside, Maggie would shiver, so I looked online to find her a sweatshirt to wear. Once it arrived, she let me put it on her and was just fine on her walks. As I continued buying her little jackets and sweaters, I realized she loves wearing clothes! I usually only put clothes on her when we are going out, and she's very social, so I think that's why she's excited to put something on.

Maggie loves meeting new people. She will let the kids in the neighborhood pet her, and when we walk near the hospital, she will let anyone standing outside pet her. She also knows when someone compliments her. As soon as she hears someone say she is pretty or cute, she will walk right up to them and either sit by them or put her paws on them like she's trying to give them a hug.

It may sound crazy, but Maggie reminds me a lot of a human. I'll give you a few examples. When Maggie is at home, she likes looking out the window, so I put a chair by the window for her. Well, when she's in her chair, she sits with her front paws crossed!

Then there was that day that I left my queen bee shoes at the door. I always take my shoes off at the door, so that's not unusual. What made it funny is Maggie came over to where my shoes were and put her paw on the shoe with the image of the crown! I think she believes she runs our house (she might a little)!

Finally, there was the time my good friend Nicky gave Maggie a shirt with bacon on it. Maggie loves bacon, and the shirt fit perfectly, so I told her to smile so we could send Aunt Nicky a photo, and she did!

Maggie smiling for Aunt Nicky!

However, with all the good qualities she has, there are a few I hope to improve over time. Maggie can be aggressive. She doesn't like other dogs all the time, and she can be jealous. If I am showing love to another pet, she will try to chase that dog away. She's even tried to stop other owners from petting their own dogs. She's a mess! However, even with the bad, Maggie isn't going anywhere. I love her, and we will live life together as long as we can!

I gave Maggie her very first birthday party on her third birthday. By that time, we had been together for about a year and a half. I invited over Tiffany and LuLu. Tiffany is one of my best friends, and LuLu is Maggie's best friend! I had pink glittery cowboy hats for the girls to wear, as well as fancy birthday cookies. I also sent LuLu home with a goodie bag! They seemed to have fun!

Maggie is a reminder to me daily that all of my dreams before my diagnosis weren't crushed. I can still accomplish some of them. And the most important lesson I've learned from having Maggie is all dreams don't have to be big for you to celebrate once you've achieved them.

Getting a pet is a very simple thing to do. Many people have pets, some more than one pet. So, it's not a grand achievement. However, it was a goal that I set for myself, so it is worthy of celebration. And that's what I want to encourage you to do, celebrate the small things.

If your goal is to workout once a week and you achieve it, celebrate. If your goal is to learn how to cook healthier meals and you achieve it, celebrate. You can even celebrate by writing down a list of goals you want to accomplish. Whether big or small, celebrate yourself and the success you have made. Give yourself a pat on the back, order takeout from your favorite restaurant, catch a movie with a friend. Just celebrate! And you'll find this act will boost your outlook on life, give you the confidence to see that you can still achieve things and push you toward accomplishing more!

Anything I accomplish is great, and Maggie has definitely been one of the most rewarding accomplishments so far! Another accomplishment I'm proud of is becoming involved with acting.

Begin Now

What have you accomplished since your life-changing event?

Chapter 10:
Lovin' the Drama

It was 2013, and I was volunteering for the Kids College 101 Workshops at church. I was in the middle of a conversation with one of the speakers, Mr. Norman, when he asked me if I was an actor. Now, he probably asked me this because I can be very animated when I speak. I told him I had been in a couple of things, but that was a long time ago. He explained his wife was looking for a lead female for a play she wrote, and I was invited to their next rehearsal to read the role.

During that rehearsal, I rambled on and on (the character I was reading talked a lot), and by the end of the rehearsal, I was offered the role. I was excited about the opportunity! I hadn't really ever thought seriously about acting, but I really liked Mr. Norman and his wife, Lou, and I knew it would be fun working with them.

And I was right! The rehearsal process for the show went smoothly. I had space, as an actor, to add to the character, and most of our rehearsals were at their home, so there was always good food present, and we usually hung out together afterward. In the end, I was able to do the character justice on stage. I remember not having any trouble memorizing my lines, and there were many of them! My character was based on a real woman living in Louisville. I got to meet her, and she was very proud of my delivery. Mrs. Lou also commented on how I memorized every word of the script. I remember telling her that I told myself I had to memorize every line so that they would give me another chance to act in one of their future productions! We had a cast party, and I made a gift for everyone. I had such a great time. Not only was I doing something that seemed easy to me, but I ended up finding a new family as well.

It wasn't long after the production ended that Lou began asking me to act in other productions she was putting on. I was part of a few small skits at different churches, and then the next full production I was cast in with Mrs. Lou was "Is My Wife Crazy or Is It Me?" The role was challenging because my character lost her daughter and was also having problems in her marriage, both of which I didn't have any personal experience with. There was a point in the play where my character was sitting alone with her daughter's backpack, realizing she wouldn't see her again and being very upset, close to tears. What helped me get through the performance was the fact that the other actors were amazing, and they helped push me to do my best. At the end of that production, a marriage and family therapist approached me and asked me if I was from New York. I told her I was a local actor, and she proceeded to tell me that not only did I do a great job, but exactly what happened on stage is what she sees in her office with different families. Even more so than that, a couple from the audience came up to us afterward and shared that what we portrayed on stage was their story. They had lost their daughter tragically and then almost broke up as a couple. They thanked us for the performance. And that's one of the things I've grown to love about theatre. You never know who you're going to meet or how your performance will impact the audience. Throughout the next three years, I became very close to Mr. Norman and Mrs. Lou, acting with them every chance I got.

In 2016, I decided to branch out and see if I could be cast in roles with other community theatres. I saw that Faith Works Studios was holding auditions for Akeelah and the Bee, so I decided to try out. Even though most of the roles were for kids, there were a few for adults that I thought I would be good at. I really wanted the role of the older woman. During my rehearsals for my audition, I channeled my inner Cicely Tyson. On the day of my audition, I did well and eventually found out I was cast in two small roles, the pronouncer and TV host. I was excited to work with Faith Works Studios because of one of the owners, Rush Trowel.

I had looked up to Rush for quite some time and had been in several of his productions. However, those productions were based out of my church, so even though he helped with them, they weren't productions under his company name. This was my opportunity to show him my talent and hopefully have more opportunities to work with him in the future.

During rehearsals, Rush and our stage manager would use a lot of theatre lingo, and we would do theatre warm-ups. This was my first time working with someone with a heavy background in acting, and I was enjoying learning all of these new things. Rush was also a stickler for memorizing scripts verbatim, so I was glad that was something I was good at!

Once the run of Akeelah and the Bee was over, I went up to Rush and thanked him for the opportunity. He responded by telling me I was good and that he planned on using me more. And he did!

The following year I was cast as "Daughter" in Shakin' the Mess outta Misery. In this production, I was the main character! My character was reminiscing on her childhood and the women in her life who helped shape the woman she became. This production was held at a local church, and we had a good turnout! Now up until this point, I was really starting to enjoy acting. All of my experiences were very fun and memorable, and I made many new friends in the process. There were definitely struggles with trying to ensure I was being the character and being able to dissect the script. However, as long as I was putting in the hard work, I always came out doing the character justice on stage in the end.

Later that year, Rush asked me if I would be interested in stage management. He said I had the qualities to be a good stage manager, and once he explained the position to me, I decided to give it a try. Never again! Being a stage manager is exactly like babysitting adults who do not do what you tell them to do. I had to call or email and remind everyone of rehearsals. I had to call people when they weren't at rehearsal to see where they were. I also functioned as Rush's assistant. I was always being sent to find his phone or write notes about the rehearsal. It was absolutely miserable!

I know many people may love stage management, but it just didn't fit my personality. I grew up in a household where I was told what to do all the time, and I didn't have much of a say so. Being a stage manager took me right back to my childhood, and I felt like I didn't have any power. And I hated that feeling. Now the good news was the cast thought I was a good stage manager, and one person even told me I was the best stage manager they had ever had. So that did make me feel good. However, when Rush would ask me if I wanted to stage manage afterward, my answer was always no!

In 2018, Rush cast me in Mufaro's Beautiful Daughters as the storyteller. Later that year, I was the narrator in an Easter production at my church. Now, both of these roles are very significant.

Do you remember earlier when I spoke about my voice and how it made me sad sometimes because I could no longer sing, and that was part of my identity? Well, when I began acting with Rush, he put me in roles because of my voice. My voice was the reason I was the storyteller and narrator. Here I was, not liking the sound of my voice because I thought it was limiting me (not allowing me to sing) when in actuality, it was allowing me to have opportunities I wouldn't have had otherwise. Just like that, one of the things I didn't like about myself became something I learned to appreciate. Have you heard the saying, "When God shuts a door, He opens a window?" Well, that's how I felt. Yes, opportunities that I loved were gone, but in their place were budding new dreams and goals that were totally feasible for me in my new body. I feel confident in saying it was only my diagnosis of lupus that allowed me to have some of the experiences I've had. And this is where we start to talk about mindset again.

Even though lupus brought pain and disappointment, good came from my diagnosis as well. At first, when I was in the hospital and feeling horrible, I couldn't see how any good

would possibly come as a result of my diagnosis since all the changes that lupus brought were seen as negative to me. However, it was only in the process of being determined to still accomplish my goals that I realized some of the things I felt were negative at first are now positives. Having all my hair fall out made me try a new hairstyle that I would have never tried otherwise. Gaining all of that weight helped me appreciate what someone is going through who is struggling with their weight. Having my new voice opened up doors to roles I wouldn't have received with the voice I was born with. Whatever happens to you in life, don't stop looking for the positive! I promise it's there. You may not see it on the first day or even in the first month, but you will see it. It will open your eyes to all of the possible new things, despite the life event that happened to you.

After both of those opportunities, in 2019, I was cast in "For Colored Girls" as Lady in Yellow. It seemed every opportunity I was given to work with Rush helped me develop more as an actor because I would be cast in roles that weren't anything like me. Lady in Yellow is a great example of this. Even though I only had one name, I played multiple roles. One role was that of a promiscuous teen who loved to dance. Another of a battered woman who contracted AIDS from her lover. So I was doing much more research to be sure I was believable on stage.

When I wasn't on stage, I began helping Emily, Rush's wife and co-owner of Faith Works Studios, with the box office. I wouldn't answer the phone, but I would sell tickets and help with concessions during intermission. The best compliments I've received so far have been from people who saw me at the box office and were disappointed because I wasn't in the show, and they enjoyed seeing me on stage. It felt good to know people were excited to see me perform. It was rather shocking because I didn't realize people liked me that much. Now, I have heard plenty of times that I'm a great actor, but to be disappointed I wasn't on stage seemed like a new level of admiration to me. When I wasn't helping Emily at the box office, I began helping her in the costume shop.

I thought the costume shop was fun. I liked learning how to use the sewing machine and the surging machine. I knew how to hand sew because my grandma taught me in elementary school, so I had some skills. However, I wasn't using them consistently, so being in the shop not only added to the list of my sewing abilities but gave me space to do something that I learned I like doing. Sewing takes patience and precision, and those are skills I have. Also, sewing was relaxing. We usually had music on and snacks. Working with Rush, Emily, and the rest of the crew of Faith Works started becoming like a family to me. I began to miss them in between shows.

During the summer of 2019, I landed an academic counselor position at the University of Louisville. I told myself once I began working that I would eventually take courses since we only pay a fraction of the tuition costs. And when the fall semester rolled around, I decided obtaining a second bachelor's degree in theatre arts was a good option for me. Up until this point, I didn't have any formal theatre arts training, and I believed formal training would make me better at my craft. So I decided to enroll in classes for the spring semester. I took costume construction course and a course about cultural diversity in performance.

Right before classes began, I was cast in "Girl's Trip." It was a script about four best friends who decide to take a road trip and end up getting on each other's nerves. My mom had moved back to Louisville by this time. She had never seen me act in anything, although she'd heard from our other family members that I was talented. Her schedule allowed her to make one of the performances, and she thought I did a great job. As for myself, I rarely curse. However, the character I played had some choice words for her friends toward the end of the play. I remember being on stage and hearing my mom gasp when I began cursing. Even in rehearsals, the cast loved hearing me curse because it was out of my character.

Now that it's 2020, theatre is still a big part of my identity. As I'm writing this memoir, I just found out I'll be auditioning for "Clue" with Faith Works Studios, and I will be the assistant costume designer for an upcoming show in the fall. I've also been cast in an Easter production at my church.

I have big dreams with acting. It's something I'm planning on doing for the rest of my life. I'd like to do some work in professional theatres and even be in a movie or TV series. If I'm going to dream, I may as well dream big! And you should too!

However, don't stop at dreaming big. Learn to look at yourself in a new way. And while you are busy discovering the new you, pay close attention to the parts of yourself that you gained because of the experience you went through. If you are anything like me, it could be that one of the things you gained from your experience that you are struggling with is what you need to embrace to see all the new possibilities before you. You have so much more to accomplish in your life! This is just your beginning!

And speaking of dreaming big, I think the biggest dream I have accomplished to date has been opening my business, Unfurgettable Jewelry.

Begin Now

What talents and hobbies do you have that are better now that you have gone through your life-changing event?

CHAPTER 11:
UNFURGETTABLE JEWELRY

One thing that I haven't told you about Maggie is she loves jewelry. When I first got her, anytime I would put her collar on, I would tell her to come get her jewelry. Now, her collars aren't fancy with jewels or anything. Since Maggie likes being pretty, I would just call her collar jewelry. After doing this a few times, I realized Maggie might actually enjoy wearing a necklace and decided to make her something when I had some free time.

I woke up one morning, and it just hit me—I needed to start a jewelry business for pets. At first, I thought it was a silly idea. I knew Maggie would love it, but I wasn't sure about other dogs. And it didn't make me feel confident when I told people my idea, and they laughed at me.

However, when I mustered up the courage to let my sisters know, they were encouraging. Melissa even said it was the perfect business for me! And she was right! I love dogs, and I love jewelry. I'm good at picking out jewelry for others, making sure I learn their style so they get pieces that they'll love. Most of the time, for Christmas, my mom and sisters ask me to buy them jewelry. So, with the good wishes of my family, I knew it was time to move forward and make this thought an actual business.

The first thing I did was see if there were any free jewelry classes so I could brush up on my jewelry-making techniques. I was able to find a local store that had one month of free classes left. They were getting rid of all their jewelry supplies to make room for more crafts. So not only was I able to receive help on techniques to make jewelry but all of the supplies I purchased at the beginning of this journey were really cheap! During this class, I made my first piece, which I later titled "The Original." I made it for Maggie so she could have pieces to wear when we were out and about to help promote my business.

The second thing I did was look online to see who in my area helps individuals with starting a business, and I found the Small Business Development Center. I set up a meeting with one of their representatives, and he gave me some helpful tips and tools on what I should focus on first. He said I needed to start thinking about who my audience would be and how much I would sell my products for. Afterward, I definitely had some things to think about. However, the first thing I wanted to do was create my logo.

I'm a visual person and figured if I created my logo first, it would give me the confidence to keep moving forward even if people laughed because my logo would be awesome, just like I intended my products to be. It was a bit of a process. I knew I wanted something that was a play on words. After thinking of words and re-writing them so they had something to do with pets, I sent the list to my sisters, and the vote was for "unfurgettable." Once I had that, I began using free websites to get the vision of my logo into a working form. When I was finished with it, the color and script were great but I was missing a picture and I wanted the outside of the logo to look more like a dog tag instead of a cloud. At that point, a coworker told me about Fiverr, which is a company that employs folks from all over the world who can help you with almost anything related to a business. I found someone fairly quickly for the price range I was looking for, and I explained what I needed. Within a few days, I had my finished logo and the rights to it!

I received lots of compliments on the logo. When I started to ask around to see if folks thought I needed to go through the trademark process, everyone said yes and began to tell me stories about people they knew who had their logos stolen. I had worked really hard on mine and didn't want that to happen, so I decided to find a company to help me trademark my logo. I paid them to walk me through the first few steps of the process. Once I realized I could get through the process on my own, I stopped using the company and did the rest by myself.

The whole trademark process took longer than I expected. I knew I didn't want to start the business without my trademark because the logo was my business name, and I wanted to be sure it was mine and protected. I wanted to be prepared so I could start strong and not have to stop selling or close in a few months because I didn't plan well enough. So while I was going through the trademark process, I participated in two workshops that helped new business owners.

I found out about the first workshop through one of my good friends. Her friend, who was a successful business owner, was leading the workshops. Once she met me and learned what I was doing, she let me sit in during their meetings. Each speaker had information about the different aspects of having a business. For example, we got to hear from a lawyer about how to write contracts. Those who paid to participate also got to pitch their business ideas to people in the community and get feedback on how to make their pitches better. Since I was a guest of the program, I couldn't pitch my idea in front of the panel, but I was able to participate in everything else.

I met with Angelique, the young woman leading the entrepreneurship program, one Sunday. I just wanted to pick her brain a little more about my business ideas. We met for popsicles, and then she graciously followed me home so I could show her some of my products.

Angelique said my products were really nice. She suggested ways I could lower costs, and we decided to take some photos of Maggie wearing different necklaces. She definitely did not cooperate! However, we got some outstanding shots with Angelique's phone. Take a look!

Maggie wearing "The Original"

Maggie wearing a fabric piece I created.

The second program was for people who wanted to sell online. Where I live, our government has a partnership with Etsy. I was afforded the opportunity to sit in some courses for new business owners. While there one night, I was told of a man who worked at the local library that was really good at helping people find market data regarding their business. So when I called the library to see when he would be working again, I was told he would be in that weekend.

When I spoke to him about finding data about other people in our area selling jewelry and the reasons people buy presents for their pets, he told me he thought I had a good idea and told me about the Etsy program. I thanked him for the information and looked into it further once I got home.

The entrepreneur partnership with Etsy was for small business owners who wanted to sell online. The program was free. You just had to apply. On the application, they wanted to know why I wanted to be a part of the program, what I was selling, and if I had the time to commit, and they wanted to see pictures. I submitted everything and waited to hear back.

It was a few days later that I discovered I had been accepted. I took part in about six classes that not only helped me think about things a business owner should think about— how to keep books, how to find out how much you are spending on your products, how to determine the cost of your products, how to take good pictures, etc., but the program also talked specifically about selling on Etsy and also gave every participant free listings to get started.

I did well in the course, and I was able to learn a lot. It seemed to be a perfect fit for me because I was sure I would begin selling on Etsy since that's where people go for handmade crafts. And I wanted to sell there because it was cheap! I eventually purchased a web domain and linked it to my Etsy account to make it easier for people to type on my website.

Now, while I was going through the process for the trademark and attending the Etsy course, I was working on my products. The main product I wanted to sell was custom necklaces for pets, specifically dogs and cats. This is why my logo has a picture of the side profile of a dog and cat combined with a funky necklace. I was very interested in the custom necklaces because that would allow me to get to know the pets that would wear my product and design something specifically for them, like I would buy jewelry for my family members in their own styles. I also felt this would be a good way to name each piece. I really wanted each piece to have a name to add to the uniqueness of what I was doing.

Additionally, I wanted to do other types of jewelry just in case someone didn't want a necklace for their pet. Even though I had many ideas, I only wanted to push out one idea at a time for two main reasons. The first was it was just me, so I needed to be sure I could handle the demand of filling orders. The second was because I didn't take out any loans to start my business.

Looking back, it probably would have helped to take out a small business loan. However, even though I could have, I didn't want to go into debt by starting the business, so I did everything out of pocket. I felt this was something I was destined to do, so I figured things would work out. My sisters also gave me money and bought me beads.

As I began to talk to my sisters and close friends about my product ideas, I asked them to try different products on their pets to help me figure out how big to make my small, medium, and large sizes. Once I confided that I had an idea for an interesting take on the bow tie, one of my friends told me I could have her sewing machine that she wasn't using. I told her I needed to find someone with a sewing machine and ask them to borrow it so that I could make my bow ties. Well, my friend said she couldn't find her sewing machine, so she went out and purchased one for me! And it was a good thing she did because I definitely ended up needing it!

Even though I had been given a sewing machine, I didn't know how to use one. When I asked my friends who knew how to sew, none of them had the time to teach me, which was okay. I tend to be very busy and cannot do all of the things that people want me to do. So, I figured while I learned how to use the machine, I could ask around for a good seamstress and pay her to make them for me. I went to meet a local seamstress I was told about, and she was really nice. I told her my idea, and she loved it. She ended up creating a prototype for me that I used to show people what I was thinking about. However, I had to stop working with her because once I showed her work to my friends who knew how to sew, they told me that what she had done wasn't good quality.

So, I decided that I needed to learn how to sew myself so that I could have the quality I wanted. That is one of the reasons the first class I took at U of L was the costume construction class.

It wasn't until September 2019 that I finally received my trademark notice. The process was finally over, and not a minute too late because I had decided to launch my shop on my birthday, October 1st. This way, I wouldn't have a hard time remembering the date!

Me officially launching Unfurgettable!

After the launch, I had my first sales within that month! I had been talking about selling necklaces for the past two years, so plenty of friends were excited to buy a custom piece finally. After each sale, I did a spotlight on each pet on my Instagram business page. I had over 100 followers within the first month!

As I am writing this memoir, I am continuing to make necklaces for cats and dogs, and I'm having so much fun! I am looking forward to finishing my sewing class to begin making my bow ties. I am looking into having my products sold in local stores. I also want to start participating in local fairs and street markets. I am open to new ideas and see nothing but good coming from my efforts. The sky's the limit!

So what's my motivational plug for this chapter? You'll never know how far you can reach if you don't stretch your arm. If someone had told me while I was in the hospital that I would eventually start my own business, I would not have believed them. I might have even laughed at them. At that time, I was worried about my surgery and feeling better, and I was still struggling with my diagnosis. My mind was constantly on my pain and problems.

It wasn't until I could move past those things that my vision was clear enough to realize I could conquer any dream I set my mind to. Would I have still created the business if I didn't have lupus? Maybe. However, that doesn't matter. What matters is that I worked hard to achieve every dream I thought of. What matters is that I didn't let anyone's negative thoughts about my abilities stop me. What matters is that I am still here, taking my meds, determined to keep a positive outlook on life.

Now is the time to tell yourself no more excuses. No more telling yourself that you can't do something you want to do. No more letting others discourage you. No more sitting on the sideline while others are living their best life.

You can make up your mind to have a positive mindset. You can smile through the hard times. You can reach your dreams. I'm depending on you. I'm rooting for you. I support you. You can do this!

BEGIN NOW

What's a dream that you have that others told you isn't possible for you to achieve?

CONCLUSION: WHAT'S YOUR MINDSET?

Thank you for taking the time to walk with me through my lupus diagnosis and life afterward. Even though you may have gone through a life event that you feel has changed your life drastically, with a positive mindset, you can still move forward and accomplish your goals.

Along my journey, I found the enemy I needed to conquer was the inner me. Being diagnosed with lupus and my surgeries were events that were in the past. However, my life was continuing in the present. And I still had more to do.

Would I let a few events that were already over influence me for the rest of my life? Or would I choose to keep moving forward by working on my mindset? Now I'm not saying the effects of those events didn't linger because they did. I'm also not downplaying the seriousness of what happened to me because it was very serious. I am simply suggesting we have the ability to control our futures by working on our mindset.

I was diagnosed with lupus in 2007, but now I live with L.U.P.U.S.—Lives Unlocking Powerful Unexpected Strength. The illness is still there, but I don't see it the same way. I won't constantly think about the negative things my diagnosis could bring. Instead, I am choosing to live with lupus and see the good that has come because of it. And that's what this book has been about: my journey to having a positive mindset with lupus.

I had to learn how to love myself again, even though I didn't like how lupus had affected me. I had to accept that life would never be the way it was before my diagnosis. I had to be willing to search for the good even when it was barely visible. And it was my commitment to these things that allowed me to have a shift in my mindset.

Once I began to work on loving myself, I discovered I was left with more of me than what lupus had taken away. Once I stopped wishing for the impossible, that life would return to normal, I could appreciate the new changes, like my voice, that lupus had left me with. Once I stopped focusing on the negative and started looking for the good, I realized my life still had meaning, and I could accomplish not only some of my old dreams but new ones as well.

Where are you with your mindset? Are you still stuck believing that nothing good will come of your life? Or have you begun to see and appreciate the things you still have? If you feel stuck, I want to encourage you to work on shifting your mindset. Baby steps will do.

Maybe after reading this book, you will write down a list of goals that you have for yourself and ways you can still accomplish them. Maybe you will decide to join a support group to hear from others that are going through a similar situation. Maybe you will decide to wake up each morning and say one positive thing about yourself. It's all up to you.

You can create a new life for yourself. A life where you have goals and a purpose. A life where you still achieve your dreams despite what has happened to you. A life that brings a smile to your face and gives you a reason to get out of bed each morning. Your life is still worth living. You just have to choose to believe it.

As I live longer, I'm finding out that although my diagnosis of lupus brought the most pain in my life, being diagnosed was one of the best things that has ever happened to me. I learned how resilient I am and how faithful God is. I've learned to love myself in spite of my imperfections, and as I continue to grow, I've realized all of my struggles have been designed to make me into the woman I am continuously becoming. This Pamala, the woman I am today, I wouldn't trade her for anything!